# GARDEN
## for the
# SENSES

# GARDEN

## for the

# SENSES

how your garden can soothe your mind and awaken your soul

KENDRA WILSON

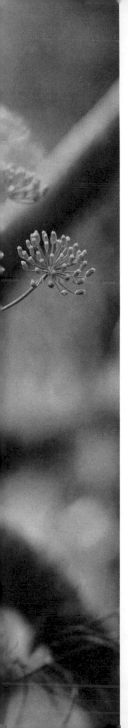

# Contents

# Introduction

The connection between gardens and happiness has long been known; cultivating plants "makes all our sences swimme in pleasure," observed garden writer William Lawson, in 1618. Today, this idea has more resonance than ever, as science tells us what we have always felt instinctively: that simple labor and uncomplicated exercise—outdoors—is good for us. The joy of creativity as we construct a garden is one byproduct; excellent food as we grow it another. In a thriving, abundant, and therefore beautiful garden, both mind and body can indeed swim in pleasure.

Growing for the senses is gardening for fun. Smells, tastes, colors, sounds, and textures bring in a myriad of life forms, whether flying, buzzing, hopping, or slithering, that will in turn give you a focus for your nose, mouth, eyes, ears, and hands. An increased awareness of garden senses engages the mind, and plants that appeal strongly to at least one sense are simply more interesting.

This book is about thinking more carefully about your garden and making considered choices that can lead to a better appreciation of the small things. A low-maintenance shrub chosen for its effort-free nature is all very well, and may provide a degree of privacy, but will it bring happiness? Instead, you could have a mutually supportive community of plants—each of which will appeal to one or more of your senses—that will be "low-maintenance" simply because they like the conditions your plot can provide. As they thrive, you thrive, and your garden comes to life.

# CREATING

# A SENSORY

# GARDEN

# Creating a garden for your senses

The senses—and plants that appeal to each specifically—generally overlap. Like a Venn diagram, smell and taste are intertwined, while texture engages the eyes as much as the touch receptors of the fingertips. Apples, pears, and quince seem to be designed for grasping in the palm of the human hand: a pear might look ripe on the tree, but if the stalk doesn't bend off with a snap, it needs longer. A quince, looking somewhat like an oversized yellow pear, is rock-hard, and needs heat to soften the flesh. Its scent gives quince the edge: after bringing some fruit indoors, its presence is announced by a lingering perfume. Smells of degrading are not always so pleasant: an aging cabbage gives off a kind of gas, which means it is best eaten immediately after harvesting.

Sight, smell, and touch pave the way to taste: experiencing food as it grows is a way of understanding its unhurried progression to the optimum moment of ripeness and flavor. On nurturing a radish from seed to plate, it becomes clear why some fresh food devotees will eat a salad, lightly dressed, with their fingers: they are going for the full taste-and-texture immersion.

When growing plants for one sense, an appreciation of the other four will follow. Instead of choosing a single type of rose or lily over another, go all out, growing loads. You might have chosen some because of a passion for their fragrance, but may soon realize that you prize their texture and the way they look as well. Against a wall or fence, you might grow a group of hollyhocks in a variety of colors because they are natural companions for buildings, but you'll soon become engrossed in the pollen-spilling activities of bumblebees as they crawl all over the anthers, as well as noticing how each bud slowly opens from the bottom of the plant upward. Foxgloves develop in the same way, are good in an unregulated group, and seem to be designed to fit snugly around a bumblebee, rather than the paw of a fox.

Hollyhocks bring life to railings and walls with sublime colors and prolific pollen.

It is useful to recognize beneficial bugs and insects at all stages so that you can more easily welcome them into a garden. This is a ladybug at larva stage: a profilic aphid eater.

## More is more

Gardening for the senses is about profusion, rather than precision. In a thoughtful essay on houses and gardens at the turn of the 19th century, Robert Louis Stevenson advised that, rather than try to orchestrate nature, "The gardener should be an idler," leaving well enough alone. Except, that is, in a kitchen garden: the perfect place for people who want to be busy. An area of productivity, where flowers mix freely with fruit and vegetables, is heaven for all the senses. Because diversity is so important for soil and plant health, a mixed garden—whether or not it is given the prefix "kitchen"—is a good thing to strive for, from the smallest space upward. Planting can be based on flavor, or looks, or both. Zucchini, blackberry bushes, and strawberries do a wonderful job of covering bare earth, stabilizing soil, attracting pollinators, feeding birds: there is no pressure to eat it all yourself. Abundant produce and seeds can be shared with other people;

generosity is good for you, and is said to be one of the keys to happiness. When you begin to get out of the habit of throwing everything in the trash, the compost heap is a happy destination for garden or kitchen waste.

## Slow down

Observing the cycle of life is about slowing down, and a micro-view of the world is a way of engaging all the senses. Recognizing beneficial insects that do not advertise their virtues as easily as bees and butterflies is one way of letting go and stepping back, confident in the knowledge that predators were keeping "pest" populations in check long before insecticide was invented. Seeing your outside space up close brings new meaning to small gardens, driveways, and even rubble. If you see local wildflowers and self-seeded plants as useful ground cover, rather than nuisance weeds, then there will be more to look at as well as to hear, with the

A gloriously mixed-up garden attracts a greater diversity of insects and soil microbes.

The result of tolerating brambles is blackberries for you, plus habitat, food, and a breeding ground for insects. The result of tolerating caterpillars is, of course, butterflies and moths, and pollenated flowers.

earliest spring bumblebees joined later by hoverflies, ladybugs, and parasitic wasps (which also have their uses). Insects and a bit of leaf cover attract birds, while impermeable paving does not.

Gardens and landscape merge when your senses are alive; on noticing the activity in your garden, the rest of your neighborhood will become more intriguing. The exhilaration of spring is intensified by a great unleashing of birdsong, by the bedroom window, in every tree. If you see your outdoor space as a concentration of the wider landscape, it is easier to learn from both, by looking and listening.

### Go with nature's flow

Particular scents mark the rituals of a season's progression: "lilac time" can be enjoyed in the hedgerows as well as in the more luxuriant garden varieties. If you look at how lilac, or rhododendron, or viburnum grows in untamed spaces, and adapt this to your garden, you will avoid the dilemma of housing a rather dull shrub in too prominent a place for the majority of the year: instead it will play an integral part in your own landscape, no matter how small. In this way, you will leap the fence and see (to steal Horace Walpole's 18th-century description of landscaper William Kent) that all nature is a garden.

### Choose carefully

The key to keeping your own garden under control is in the editing. Perhaps buddleia, inhabitant of railroad tracks, is not your favorite plant, but if you find a cultivar in a deeper purple, or with a more refined scent, you might consider allowing one to take up residence in your garden. The butterflies that flock around buddleia and keep a garden in motion will not mind either way. Wildflowers are wonderful when mixed with highbrow flowers that you have chosen for their striking beauty or glamorous fragrance. Texture is important here, with "wildies" taking

Ornamental tree sweet gum *Liquidambar styraciflua* brings fall drama into larger gardens.

Bees fit into foxgloves perfectly and are fascinating to watch, if you allow yourself to stop, as they go about their business.

their place among more dominant outlines and leaf shapes. A hierarchy of planting is important, guided by the senses. Your eyes as well as your horticultural experience will guide you. As Vita Sackville-West noted, "I don't like to see ground-elder poking up its ugly leaf among irises." One is ugly, the other beautiful... but that is as much to do with the habit of the uncontrollable versus the dependable.

Strong leaf shapes by a path's edge capture the attention when flowers are still waking up: mottled, shiny *Arum italicum*, outlined edges of *Geranium phaeum*, dainty-looking yet tough epimedium. Creating paths that are wide enough for a wheelbarrow, but not much more, makes everything that is spilling over more noticeable. By midsummer, you will be pushing your way through. Covering every bit of bare earth has the advantage of protecting it; growing plants en masse gives them safety in numbers when a summer storm comes along to mess it all up.

In *Cider with Rosie*, Laurie Lee recalls his mother's cottage garden in Slad, Gloucestershire, home to "such a chaos of blossom as amazed the bees and bewildered the birds of the air." The garden's bounty would decorate the inside of the cottage before being eaten or used, in the form of a bouquet of rhubarb or a posy of herbs.

### ... and relax

A garden for the senses is a garden with atmosphere; it tolerates some nettles, since they provide important habitat, and some thistles, for their nectar-rich flowers. When your senses are more highly attuned, you will have a greater enjoyment of all manner of plant life, rather than only conventionally approved horticulture. The potential of close-at-hand taste, texture, smell, and nourishment for the eyes and ears is so great, that when people lack one sense, there is compensation. When you find yourself gardening after dark, you'll know you are hooked.

Ox-eye daisies, red campion, columbine, fennel, and lamb's ears mix well with other wild flowers.

# THE
# SENSES

# TOUCH

The act of touch, when gardening, is often a question of choice: are you going to grasp that stalk of comfrey with its million little hairs, one of which is bound to get under your skin, or are you going to put on sturdy gloves first? In the case of euphorbia, with its toxic sap, it would be foolish not to.

But the physical handling of plants is how a gardener gets to know them, and it's also a way of recognizing the point of texture in a garden created for the senses—giving plants their form, structure, and movement. Toes can also do a lot of touching, given half a chance; so indulge them with thoughtful landscaping, both hard and soft, in your outside space.

Comfrey is a member of the *Boraginaceae* family, with degrees of hairiness from highly irritating green alkanet to soft, sweet forget-me-not and edible (yet hirsute) borage. Comfrey 'Bocking 14' is sterile and makes an excellent plant food and soil conditioner.

# To touch or
# not to touch

An old wisteria, its twisted, serpentlike trunk dripping with racemes of amethyst flowers, adds gravitas to a property. The act of planting one is a step toward permanence, and some kind of grandeur. But the relationship goes both ways: in order for a wisteria to do what you want it to do, you need to become intimate with the whippy shoots, the masses of leaves, and every season's new, astonishing growth. You need to climb a ladder twice a year, and, with your hands, work your way over the entire plant, making informed decisions about where to cut and what to tie in. This is a job best done without gloves. You could pay someone else to do it, but why give them all the fun?

Pruning a woody plant is a kind of restoration, one which can be as satisfying as peeling back the layers of a house, and improving its functionality. It's better than that, though, because the pleasure is in the process as much as the result; in the handling of plants, rather than wallpaper. Gloves are obviously optional, but it's rewarding to take them off when they are not strictly necessary. Prodding, squeezing, plucking bits of your garden, with bare hands, is how you get to know it; pulling out the easy weeds (such as groundsel, which offers little resistance) as you go around, is part of the act of looking. Grasping blades of grass in a gravel garden and yanking them out is how you notice other more interesting things that are coming up, not all of which will be weeds. Grab a kneeling pad; stay a while.

Part of the appeal of Frances Hodgson Burnett's book *The Secret Garden* is in the sympathetic fettling: "It wouldn't seem like a secret garden if it was tidy," says Mary Lennox. The enchantment of the garden lies in textures: the door swinging open under a curtain of ivy, the old roses tangled

To flower at its best, wisteria's copious green growth is best tackled twice a year, with bare hands and pruning shears.

in the grass, hanging from trees, climbing over and falling off walls. It's also about the soil, and plunging hands into newly dug earth; this is how Mary befriends the robin, who shows her the old garden key, revealed in freshly turned-over soil. Dirt under the fingernails is a badge of honor for gardeners; it's difficult to commune with fresh homemade compost when it is held at arm's length on a spade, or by gingerly picking it up with a new pair of gardening gloves.

## Do touch

Deterred from an early age by the admonishment: "Don't touch!," we tend to leave plants alone between seasonal interventions. And yet, a garden can be surprisingly soft, especially these days, when grasses are so prized. There is a world of fluffiness out there, from silvery-white "rabbit-tail" flowerheads of *Pennisetum villosum*, to plumes of *Stipa tenuissima* and silky tassels of *Miscanthus sinensis*. Grasses such as *Hakonechloa macra* and taller *Sesleria autumnalis* form irresistible shag-pile rugs, with a sideline in weed suppression. In shadier, more sheltered areas, ferns can also be tough but soft, such as lady fern (*Athyrium filix-femina*) and the soft shield ferns *Polystichum setiferum*.

The noticeably large and soft leaves of great mullein have been used in days gone by for lining shoes (its folk names make a long list, including "feltwort" and "old man's flannel"). Silver-green lamb's ear (*Stachys byzantina*) makes an informal edging and is absurdly soft, like pussy willow (the pollinated catkins of goat and gray willow). Catnip is pleasant to stroke, especially for cats, but, better still, Russian sage (*Perovskia* 'Blue Spire'), in the same purple-silver spectrum, has stalks and calyxes that are as felted and wired as pipe cleaners,

Handle with care:
viper's bugloss
and thistle make a
beautiful, untouchable
combination.

standing up to wind and lasting through winter as pale ghosts. A tender alternative, with scarlet velvet stalks and calyxes (and red flowers to match), is *Salvia confertifolia*.

Moss has been inexplicably demonized in the west, but different mosses placed together with skill by Japanese gardeners are velvety, bumpy, quilted. Mosses are brightened by a stream or mini-waterfall; the cloud-shaped mounds have a mutually flattering relationship with the electric-red or pea green leaves of *Acer palmatum*, and bristles of miniature pines. Ancient woodlands offer hairier mosses, thriving in the half-light on trees and logs. Stroke some; it feels like an ungroomed Old English Sheepdog.

### Spines, stings, and slug slime

The open countryside, with its armies of wildflowers and "rank" weeds, can be a scarier place to brush against. Poisonous hemlock has similar leaves to soft, feathery cow parsley, and its branching umbels resemble those of hogweed. Is it safe to touch any of them? (Yes to cow parsley, no to hogweed, giant hogweed, and hemlock.) The scenery loses its fresh green look after midsummer, when towering nettles hang with seeds, and wild plants are not just laden with stings and prickles, they seem as though they could easily tangle around you and pull you under. For anyone straying off the trodden path, the countryside becomes more physical; it reaches to touch you, even as you try to avoid touching it. Thomas Hardy describes this loss of civility in *Tess of the D'Urbervilles*: "She went stealthily as a cat through this profusion of growth, gathering cuckoo-spittle on her skirts, cracking snails that were underfoot, staining her hands with thistlemilk and slug-slime..."

Blackthorn, as the name implies, makes a dark silhouette with long, gothic spines. It was a bewitched *Prunus spinosa* that linked arms with a supercharged bramble to cause a century of havoc for suitors in *Sleeping Beauty*. Blackthorn is a changeling in early spring, with the appearance of intense clusters of white flowers, before fresh green leaves. Thorns are far more beautiful than chain-link fence, and hawthorn makes an excellent impenetrable hedge, with the bonus of blossom and berries. For a magical combination of thorn on thorn, the broad-leaved cockspur thorn *Crataegus persimilis* 'Prunifolia', flowering in spring, can be paired with *Rosa* 'Scharlachglut', its abundance of scarlet-crimson flowers in summer followed by autumn rose hips shaped like urns.

Some of the most romantic old roses have buds that are so textured with prickly fuzz that they are known as moss roses, while the winged thorn rose, *R. sericea* 'Pteracantha', sports translucent red thorns in winter, like ropes of shark's fins. The red stems are a forest of prickles. *Rosa spinosissima* is possibly not the spiniest rose of all, although its hips are alluringly black, instead of the usual red. One of the most eccentric prickly roses, *R. roxburghii*, has peeling bark and round hips that look like buckeye casings, completely covered in prickles and of little use to anyone, let alone birds.

*Rosa sericea* 'Pteracantha', the winged thorn rose, has simple white blooms but comes into its own in winter and early spring when its stems are backlit by the sun.

## Using your feet more

A chamomile lawn is a lovely idea if you like the smell of chamomile, and don't mind pulling out the grass that it fatally attracts. Thyme is also hard-wearing but is best grown between paving, giving bare feet an opportunity to experience hot slabs interspersed with cool, creeping thyme. A challenge—that pays off in summer—is to plot a path around a garden that is navigable with bare feet, from the back door to the hot spots, without having to walk on gravel or anything else that might slow a person down.

Children love lawns, which come into their own with ball games, and they are also useful for entertaining. A lawn is perfect for a party, but there must be no hint of damp and it is only after sustained warm weather that grass is really dry enough to sit or lie on. In northern climes, a planned barbecue or picnic is an open invitation for rain. In which case, by the time goal posts and trampolines are no longer a feature, there is little sense in keeping a large lawn, with grass mown lifelessly short. A more tactile alternative would be to have just some of it shorn, still good for running over in hot weather, feet pounding on hard earth. But these areas could comprise paths, that lead to seating areas, which would be surrounded by something a bit looser, and taller, than green grass.

Filling the cracks between paving is best started off by you, with a view to letting nature do its artful spreading. Exposed soil is an invitation for random weed seeds to find a home there.

# Soil

Being caught without gardening gloves when something urgent needs doing is no bad thing. Gardening without gloves is not for everyone; it requires more care, and time, but gardening slowly has its benefits: the longer you spend with soil, the more you increase exposure to its microbes.

Under-examined soil microbes have gained respect in recent years due to their role in helping plants to sequester carbon from the atmosphere. *Mycobacterium vaccae* is known to have a visceral effect on people as well as plants. By getting it into our systems, we aid our own gut bacteria population in activating the brain to release more serotonin. Higher levels of serotonin positively impact mood, cognitive function, sleep, and digestion, while strengthening the immune system. The latter, when going well, is linked to better mental health.

Just inhaling *M. vaccae* is helpful, and activities that will involve aerobic exercise while handling soil—such as turning compost, mulching or muck spreading, and planting trees—will improve its uptake. *M. vaccae* is also present in food we might grow. Young children have the right idea about earth, dirt, and mud; an early—and ideally, long-term—exposure to *M. vaccae* sets the body on the path to stronger immunity.

Forego your gardening gloves and mess about in the dirt: soil is full of beneficial bacteria that contribute to our physical and mental wellbeing.

### Underground activity

Land that is blanketed with plants, with little soil showing, is actively storing carbon, keeping it out of the atmosphere. By protecting and enriching soil, we can improve a plant's rate of photosynthesis, and capacity to take more carbon from the air. Around the roots of plants, networks of microorganisms feed off the carbon sugars produced by photosynthesis and, in exchange, they feed plants with minerals. A rich diversity of plants increases the vigor of microbe populations.

# The science of touch

When we touch something, or something touches us, we feel it through specific receptors in our top layers of skin. These respond to varying sensations such as temperature, pressure, or pain. Their gathered information is signaled to the central nervous system—in other words, the brain and spinal cord, in that order. When a sting, bite, or burn is involved, the alert will bypass the brain and rush straight to the spinal cord, resulting in a reflexive response. Only after the affected part of the body has been snatched away does the brain gather information on what has happened.

Consider a plant, which cannot move away from a source of danger. When a person lumbers over to water it, cuts pieces off it, or stands there blocking its precious light, a stationary plant prepares for the worst. Every time it is touched, by a human, by another plant, or by a herbivore, there is an intense physiological response that is part of its distress system. This expends energy, diverting it from the plant's growth. (Plants also have a mechanism for halting the distress response.) Brushing against ferns, or tying up climbers, does not lead to serious damage, but frequent touching can stunt growth.

Generally, a plant's natural inclination is to grow toward light, even if it means that—from our point of view—it develops a less desirable shape. A gardener's own inclination, especially with annuals, is to encourage a plant to be strong and stout in form rather than tall and rangy. Sweet peas, for instance, will have their growing tips pinched off after the appearance of the first true leaves, so that they become more bushy, with wide, fibrous stems, and plenty of side shoots for maximum flowers. Obviously, the plant is not able to object. The irony is that these ministrations result in tougher, stronger plants.

Sweet peas naturally grow toward light. In tying them up and pinching out their growing tips, we are literally training them to do what we want.

# All the good feels

When people choose to restrict their palette and make a color-themed garden (and not necessarily sticking to just one color—Vita Sackville-West described her world-famous "White Garden" as a "gray, white, and green garden"), texture becomes less easy to ignore. It's a good exercise, in a world of too many options, to restrict the one so that you can explore the other. In such a garden, different qualities of stems and foliage become apparent, as well as contrasts in structure and size. The next step would be a green garden. That sounds boring to people who love color, but it makes a fascinating backdrop to well-chosen materials, such as a stone trough or zinc basin, well-considered paving, or gravel into which colorful bulbs could make an annual appearance, sinking back without a trace in their dormant months.

Some vegetable leaves are so tactile that they invite prodding if not harvesting, such as seriously shiny chard, particularly when the rainbow varieties (with stems of brightest mustard yellow and shocking pink) are backlit by the rays of a low winter sun. Since chard keeps sprouting new leaves, the effect won't be spoiled by gentle picking. Just planting two types of parsley—flat French, next to decorative curly—is a lesson in texture and contrast. In an herb garden, finer-leaved bulbs mix well with spreading, aromatic mats, for instance allium drumsticks (*A. sphaerocephalon*), part claret, part green, flying over a mat of golden marjoram. The waxy blooms and glaucous, squeaky leaves of tulips coincide with late-winter vegetable shapes, such as ruffled, slightly rubbery Italian kale (cavolo nero), or satiny, deep-red radicchio.

There are trees with trunks too good not to touch. Paperbark maple (*Acer griseum*), a smallish tree with rust-colored bark, is constantly shedding, like a buffalo in spring.

The "want to touch" quality of Swiss chard is only enhanced by the intense colors of the rainbow varieties.

It is tempting to help it along every time you pass. Or perhaps you prefer something highly burnished, such as mahogany-stemmed Tibetan cherry (*Prunus serrula*), which divides neat people—who stroke it to encourage shedding—from laissez-faire people, who allow the bark to curl up and drop off on its own. The bark of sweet chestnut (more often found in woodland or larger gardens) swirls around the trunk, spiraling upward. Branches are finished with long, narrow, serrated leaves and acid-green, impossibly spiky fruits, which can be gingerly prized open to reveal silky-smooth chestnuts within—far more refined than conkers.

Winter is the best season to notice bark effects and tree shapes (with severely pollarded willow happily sprouting back in spring). It is also the season in which grassy perennial gardens justify their long buildup, not really springing into action until well after midsummer. Alliums, again, make an excellent contrast with grasses, with giant *Allium* 'Summer Drummer' standing up to massive, golden-flowered *Stipa gigantea*, or metallic *Allium christophii* running through *Miscanthus sinensis* 'Morning Light'. This combination has the advantage of lasting well into the seed-head stage of both, grass hiding the allium foliage as it shrivels. Long-lasting winter grasses include vertical *Calamagrostis* x *acutiflora* 'Karl Foerster' and fountains of *Pennisetum macrourum*. Pheasant grass enjoys a grooming: just run your hands through it, pulling out weaker strands.

In temperate gardens, grasses such as *Pennisetum macrourum* have a second act in winter, creating a long-lasting focus.

**"** Miss Bennet, there seemed to be a prettyish kind of a little wilderness on one side of your lawn. **"**

Jane Austen, *Pride and Prejudice*, 1813

# Plants for touch

## White-stemmed bramble
*Rubus cockburnianus*

It is a strange idea: a purely "decorative" bramble. However, in the depths of winter, when the eye is craving detail, or anything interesting to focus on, this white-stemmed bramble is unique. Under its ghostly pallor is an undercoat of red, which works well with the fiery stems of *Cornus sanguinea* (common dogwood) whose fresh growth, once pruned, glows red and amber. Seen from a distance, *R. cockburnianus* makes a graceful tangle.

Full sun, well-drained soil.

## Bleeding heart *Dicentra*

Dangling from arching stems, lilac pendants of *Dicentra formosa* (*formosa* meaning "beautiful") invite tickling; and a brush over its lacy, fernlike foliage. *D. cucullaria's* white flowers hang like the upside-down pantaloons of a miniature 16th-century explorer, which is why their common name is "Dutchman's breeches." Note: a more familiar plant with pink-and-white "bleeding hearts," formerly known as *D. spectabilis*, is now considered a different genus and has been renamed *Lamprocapnos spectabilis*.

These are woodland plants and need shelter, with good drainage.

## Squash and pumpkin *Cucurbita*

Edible fruits do not need to be eaten when they are this decorative, but some varieties are both ornament and food. Hard-skinned winter squashes are varyingly bumpy and intensely colored ('Red Kuri'), or smooth ('Crown Prince' with pale verdigris skin). Summer squashes are equally tactile, such as "patty pans," or curiously elongated *C. moschata* 'Tromboncino'. Growing them climbing up sturdy supports saves space and aerates the developing fruit.

Not frost-hardy, thirsty, and hungry; grow on well-prepared ground, with plenty of space.

## Pasqueflower *Pulsatilla vulgaris*

Silky, silvery buds and stems give a hint of the seed heads that last for months after the flower has gone. Pasqueflowers are memorable in bloom: only 8in (20cm) high but with large violet flowers, luminous yellow stamens, and deeply cut leaves. Flowers are cushioned with the hairy strands of the outer segments. Textures in silver-brown silk follow as the seed heads develop into sturdy spheres of long, soft fibers. A good mixer with other gravel garden plants.

Excellent drainage, full sun, can take exposure. A raised trough highlights the nodding flowers.

Clockwise from top *White-stemmed bramble, Pasqueflower, Bleeding heart.*

> **"**Beautifully detailed *Phacelia tanacetifolia*, curled and decorated like an Elizabethan coxcomb**"**

**Artichoke**  *Cynara scolymus*

"The artichoke is an edible thistle," wrote food writer Jane Grigson, before detailing "How to tackle artichokes." "Tackling" the vegetables in trepidation is how artichokes are approached by the novice, whereas old hands can show the pleasures of unpeeling the bracts of a young flower bud, and dipping them in melted butter. An artichoke in flower is a pollinator-attracting thistle. *Cynara scolymus* is grown for its wide, silver leaves, which snap easily and need plenty of space.

**Long-lived perennials, in deep, rich, fertile soil and full sun.**

**Lacy Phacelia**  *Phacelia tanacetifolia*

The term "green manure" is a little lacking in describing beautifully detailed *Phacelia tanacetifolia*, curled and decorated like an Elizabethan coxcomb. And yet that is one of its benefits: as ground cover, lacy phacelia holds nitrogen in the soil, and its low-lying, yet ferny foliage is dug into the ground (before flowering) in midsummer, with a view to improving soil fertility. It is very rewarding, however, to keep a section of flowers, so that you can wonder at their construction, while watching bees pick their way over the stamens. *Phacelia* is a self-seeding annual that is related to hairy borage, both of which will take on a welcome permanence in your garden.

**Full or partial sun, well-drained soil.**

**Dill**  *Anethum graveolens*

A charming, bright green plant when young, with gossamer leaves that are not as delicate as they look. Dill is a more ephemeral presence than fennel and its gargantuan relation, giant fennel. Instead, it quietly attracts pollinators, happily growing as a line or block in a vegetable garden, but ideally en masse, so that it can be seen. The feathery foliage and seeds are used; the acid-yellow umbels held on a goblet of stems are prized by florists.

**Moist soil, full sun. Grow away from fennel to prevent cross-breeding.**

Clockwise from top  *Dill, Lacy Phacelia, Artichoke.*

**Sea holly**  *Eryngium*

For just enough spike, but not too much (if you are wary of towering specimens such as Scotch thistle), *Eryngium* is beautifully formed and burnished. The color ranges from silver to purple, with green and blue in between, and they are natural mixers with other highly textured plants that are softer, such as grasses and herbs. In fact, they need to be grown with other things, or they flop and scratch as you go past. Bristly cones bear tiny flowers, surrounded by the highly decorative, spiny ruff.

Free-draining soil, full sun—which intensifies the colors.

**Borage**  *Borago officinalis*

The term "edible" does not always imply that something is pleasant to eat, and putting a flower head of borage in your mouth proves this. The sepals are hairy, and although the taste is pleasantly reminiscent of cucumber, it is advisable to stick to the flowers only, for textural reasons. The stems and leaves are more bristly, but are easily handled, if rough textures are what you like. Borage is a long-flowering annual; like its cousin forget-me-not, its petals—a memorable blue—pop up year after year.

Control it by pulling out unwanted seedlings.

**Dwarf conifers**  various genera

In the 1950s, these gained popularity as low-maintenance ground cover. In a shrubbery of juniper, cypress, and fir, the emphasis used to be on shape and color, but now we require movement. In recent years, "shrubby" conifers have made a comeback because of their fascinating textures, and sometimes weird silhouettes. They succeed with herbaceous perennials and big-leaved foliage plants. With evergreen grasses, they help a winter garden to retain texture when color has drained away.

Full sun to semi-shade in a sheltered position, with well-drained soil.

**Love-lies-bleeding**  *Amaranthus*

Decadent velvet flower eruptions shoot upward (*Amaranthus paniculatus*) or trail lugubriously (*A. caudatus*). *A.* 'Red Army' has deep red foliage that matches the flower, highlighting the extreme contrast in leaf smoothness and finely knobbled flower texture. Amaranth grain (seeds of mainly *A. caudatus*) is gluten free and was a key food source for Aztecs. A highly decorative addition to gardens, ranging from deep crimson to lime green and mustard yellow.

Tender, requiring full sun and well-drained soil.

Right *Love-lies-bleeding.*

# "There is a bloom to the glaucous leaves which is sensitive to touch, disappearing when rubbed"

**Yew**  *Taxus baccata*

Yew's ability to regenerate from its core, ensuring its survival over hundreds of years, is useful in gardening. Cut it back hard; it comes back. Fashion it into a peacock shape that doesn't quite work out and it will come back, ready to become a cube. All parts are highly toxic, except for the fleshy red casings holding poisonous seeds. Armed with gloves and remembering to pick up the clippings, common yew is too good to ignore, poisonous or not.

Grows in any situation, but soil must be well-drained.

**Oyster leaf plant**  *Mertensia maritima*

A fish substitute in a vegetable, oyster leaf plant is distinctly salty and fishy, and even fleshy—like an oyster. There is a bloom to the glaucous leaves which is sensitive to touch, disappearing when rubbed. They are salad leaves that resemble succulents, growing to about 8in (20cm). *Mertensia maritima* is in the *Boraginaceae* family, along with borage and comfrey, a fact that is evident in the small blue flowers. They are best picked in the morning, like all water-retentive salad leaves.

Hailing from coastal areas, they prefer sandy, very well-drained soil. They need protection from afternoon sun.

**Giant silver mullein**  *Verbascum densiflorum*

Providing two years of texture: at ground level, with large rosettes of felted silver leaves in gravel and between paving cracks in the first year; followed by the vertical spectacle of 6.6ft (2m) stems that seem to be made of thick white wool, interspersed with bright yellow flowers. Attentions from mullein moth caterpillars can result in a plant that is not dead but effectively pollarded, developing a candelabra shape. Resembling wild mullein, self-seeding *Verbascum bombyciferum* brings a relaxed air to even the most formal architecture.

Full sun, open position, poor soil, good drainage. Reliable drought plant.

## Currant  *Ribes*

Dangling like earrings from well-shaped shrubs, the small orbs complemented by vinelike leaves, currants are a pleasure to handle, as well as to look at. Opaque black currant (*Ribes nigrum*) has essential oils in its leaves. The most glassy are *R. rubrum* or red currant (in which white currants are a cultivar). Harvest currants in trusses, with the aid of scissors. If you are protecting fruits from birds, please don't harm them with netting; instead use a tightly secured, dense mesh, or fruit protection bags.

**Ideally grow by a wall in full sun or semi-shade, with well-drained soil.**

## Succulents  various genera

Grown as a collection in a wide, shallow container and topped with horticultural grit, succulents are a whole garden. And they don't just sit there; *Echeveria* sends up curved stems with dangling flowers in surprising colors, while offshoots of baby succulents are a feature of *Sempervivum*. Some are fuzzy, some are rubbery; after watering, they are fit to burst, when the limblike foliage swells.

**Succulents like desert conditions, or very free-draining soil that is 40 percent grit. They also like torrential rain, so soak indoor plants when the pots are dry.**

## Salvia  various genera

With many cultivars holding the Award of Garden Merit from the Royal Horticultural Society, this large genus of the mint family is worth exploring. Beyond the fuzzy-leaved common sage (*Salvia officinalis*), there are rich, velvety flowers, color contrasts, or strong color and texture: *S. confertiflora* lives up to its common name "red velvet sage," with coated stems and calyxes of sumptuous, fuzzy bright red and small, lipped flowers. Varyingly tender or hardy, many are invaluable for drought.

**Mulch in spring; well-drained soil.**

## Lady's mantle  *Alchemilla mollis*

The leaves display the gentle alchemy the Latin name implies, shimmering with dew drops, or holding tiny puddles of rain in the lowest point of their pleated and scalloped leaves. Lady's mantle is "superhydrophobic" (water resistant) but this is only part of her allure. Chartreuse flowers emerge from meltingly soft, unfolding leaves at the start of the season—so pretty you forget the browning and prolific self-seeding that follows. Cut them back almost to the ground, and the magic begins again.

**Useful in dry shade, but they prefer some moisture.**

Clockwise from top left  *Currant, Salvia, Succulents.*

# TASTE

A garden of flavors does not need to involve crop rotation and vegetable almanacs. There are many highly decorative plants—such as fig, quince, and rosemary—that are at home in a beautiful walled garden, but they are equally wonderful anywhere.

Happily, once you have fruit trees and long-lived herbs, you don't have to do much except enjoy their flavors, which will be fuller and brighter and therefore more luxurious than anything from a store. Some fruit trees need pruning, while others definitely do not: cherry makes its own shape and will not thank you for lopping off its limbs. So sit back, and enjoy the bounty of a relaxed garden.

Plums can be a lovely garden addition and are no trouble at all.

# Ideas on taste and flavor in a garden

The idea of a kitchen garden is a kind of paradise: the deepest, roundest flavors are yours, in exchange for some health-giving labor. But good food can also be had in the corners of an ordinary garden, and with less planning, too. Unbuyable flavors are easily attained by introducing a few good plants and then—almost—leaving them alone.

### Ambulatory eating

Alpine strawberries make the prettiest ground cover, with their fresh green serrated leaves and *kawaii*-white flowers. By June, the ultra-sweet doll's house fruits will be ready for adding to breakfast cereal, or gathered for a delicious smoothie. You might even start going out first thing in the morning just to see what to add to your breakfast. For some zing at any time of day, piquant gooseberries can be eaten on the spot. Currants—glassy baubles that are a pleasure to handle and with a spicy-fruity aroma around the leaves of black currants—only need a moment on the stove with a splash of water and sugar. Then yogurt, or even pancakes.

Planting an apple tree, of an appropriate size, is one step toward remedying the loss of flavor and nutrients that modern life has given us. It might not look like more than a stick for the first few years, but, while it is busy putting down roots, it will produce some blossoms and edible fruit. An apple needs another for pollination, so, while you are thinking about fruit trees, why not invest in some pears and plums, too? They are all members of the rose family (*Rosaceae*) and are multisensory, giving twice-yearly shows (of both blossom and fruit), seasonal sounds (buzzing and tweeting), tactility (squeeze it slightly, tug it gently: is it

Alpine, wild, or wood strawberry (*Fragaria vesca*) needs to be eaten immediately upon picking. It is highly perishable (and therefore unbuyable).

ready?), and, of course, uncompromised flavor.

When you grow fruit yourself, it is for you to judge the moment of ripeness, not for a supplier who has other concerns, such as uniformity, or sufficient robustness for risk-free transportation.

### How fresh is fresh?

Picking at the decisive moment will make or break a pea. Pods that are hard and veiny have been left too long; the pea will be edible but lack the "snap" that comes from the feel and flavor of a pea caught at the apex of freshness. Frozen peas need mint, or butter and garlic, or *something*, to make them interesting (to say nothing of their wateriness), but a bowl of un-podded peas, to be opened over a conversation or while listening to the birds, is better than even the chicest *hors d'oeuvre*. The most forward-thinking restaurants around the world are increasingly supplementing the produce that they receive from specialist growers with vegetable and fruit gardens of their own, ideally on site, and often home to niche or heritage varieties. They have recognized that seeing things growing is part of the eating experience.

A space for growing food can be as simple as a collection of large containers and—why not?—rectangles dug out of a lawn. Productivity is good-looking and doesn't have to be designed. Kitchen gardens and walled gardens imply space and formality, and, more alarmingly, a degree of organization involving charts and equipment. But if you are food-curious, yet many degrees away from buying a plot of land, a whole world of flavors can be had from growing the things that interest you right outside your kitchen door. Homemade dishes are not measured out in cellophane packets of herbs;

Flowers and fruit: mixing it all up at Worton Kitchen Garden, near Oxford in England.

there are some aromatics, say parsley or thyme, of which you can never have enough in the kitchen, while other herbs, such as basil and oregano, simply grow well.

### Enlivening salad

Lettuce is genuinely exciting when you grow it yourself: sprinkling part of a seed packet of mixed leaves onto a wide bowl of potting soil, tamping down the tiny seeds and keeping them watered produces the miracle not only of germination but of a solution to boring greens. Mixed leaves are an education in flavor, enhanced by their appearance and texture: mellow to peppery; red, green, and speckled; pointed, rounded, or frilly; soft, crunchy, or more structured. Loose-leaf varieties are best for pots: create your own salad as you pick leaves around the base of different plants, which will magically resprout for weeks at a time. Gathering these—or anything else you have planted—is not a task for rushing: it's enjoyable and to be relished, especially in summer. It doesn't have to end with that season, though. Very hardy leaves include arugula, mizuna, and spinach; they will bolt in warm weather, but will keep drawing you outdoors in winter.

All kinds of things go into a mixed salad bag bought from a dedicated grower, or onto a plate in a fancy restaurant. The presence of an oxalis leaf in an upmarket salad makes you realize you can eat some of your most annoying weeds. In centuries past, dozens of types of leaves as well as herbs and flowers would go into a single salad. Vinegar for dressing was infused with cloves, roses, or nasturtiums, with "strewings and aromatizers" (in the words of John Evelyn in his 1699 salad book *Acetaria*) involving citrus peel and juniper berries.

Buying mixed leaves from a grower, or at a farmer's market, gives a hint of the leaves that were once commonplace. Finding a mix of sorrel, red orache, chervil, and winter purslane in an early spring salad—even without identifying them—is a flavor-expanding discovery of very old textures, colors, and shapes that seem new to us.

### Running to flower

Growing edible flowers near to rows of fruit and vegetables— nasturtium, cornflower, Japanese honeysuckle, wild pansies (their cheery faces popping up here and there years after you have introduced them)—will make a salad even more enjoyable, not least for their degrees of peppery taste. If you take a more relaxed attitude toward what is palatable, then you'll be adding the small flowerheads of herbs, such as fennel and thyme, as well as flowering salad leaves such as arugula (white) and mizuna (yellow) to the bowl. If you ever buy a supermarket lettuce again, you can enhance it with ever-present flowers: pot marigold, or *Calendula officinalis*, grows all year round in a sheltered place, while wild pansies come and go.

Edible annuals are natural companions to vegetables, creating a scene in the garden that is both decorative and industrious. Some are priceless, either keeping crops healthy by deterring bugs with their smell, or attracting other pests, thereby sacrificing themselves in the act of saving a food crop for you.

French marigold, *Tagetes*, is effective in deterring whitefly and it is beautifully decked out, in crimson velvet with shots of yellow. Luxuriant nasturtiums (rich both in color and structure) attract blackfly, acting as decoys to lure them

A diverse mix of flowers will make a healthier and buzzier environment for growing fruit and vegetables.

away from French and runner beans. Other flowers, such as wild daisies, attract the beneficial insects that are crucial when fruit and vegetables need to be pollinated. Some plants just go with certain other plants, on the plate or in a greenhouse, such as tomato and basil, or rhubarb and strawberries. There are any number of combinations, but mixing it up and avoiding a monoculture confuses pests, and when your food is not struggling, it tastes better.

**Transcendental herbs**

The word "herb" indicates culinary or medicinal plants, but, really, it means any beneficial green herbage. Just as our ancestors were better and more adventurous at making salads, so they saw the potential in the new season's sticky weed (full of minerals—just add boiling water) and fresh nettle tops (for which you'll need sturdy gloves). In other cultures, weeds in a spring garden are more appreciated, with Italian nettles gathered for a spring risotto and their wild dandelion leaves sautéed or added to an *insalata*. Lemon juice, olive oil, and a bit of salt do wonders for almost any greens. In Persian cooking, part of the joy of eating is in the hours of sociable chopping: herbs are recognized as a food group, not merely a flavoring or garnish. The main ingredient of tabbouleh, for instance, is not couscous or bulgur wheat but parsley, followed by mint. And Mexicans understand herbs in more subtle ways than in guacamole, though that dip is hard to imagine without its cilantro.

Growing herbs that you have no obvious use for is worth doing because of their aromatic and decorative value, as well as their importance for insects (attracting pollinators, repelling flies). But it will open new possibilities as well.

Herbs make a natural pairing with cobblestones and paving. A labyrinth or formal pattern will provide structure to this group of aromatic plants that is not always neat.

Lovage tastes like celery; chervil has a flavor of anise; you might find that you prefer using lemon thyme or lemon verbena over common thyme or even lemon juice.

The idea of an "edible landscape" has crept into garden consciousness from its birthplace in California: plants with a culinary or herbal use are grown among those that are considered ornamental. The fact that a tunnel of squashes is as showy as an arbor of passion flowers is already known to people who like food. Mixing it all up has long been the creed of the English cottage garden and the French *potager*, and, happily, it is no longer considered incorrect to see cardoons, red orache, and amaranth in a flower border.

# Foraging

Herbal remedies are as old as the hills, but foraging for food fell out of fashion in many parts of the western world until recently. It has dovetailed with a slow reawakening to the potential of native plants and homegrown cuisine and a rediscovery of the importance of seasonal and local ingredients. In countries with a more linear relationship with food (those that didn't forget how to grow and cook), flavors that we would find unusual are taken for granted. In Italy, for example, bitter leaves are so well-regarded that they have terroir—a soil and topography where they thrive and for which a region is known—in the same way as wine or cheese.

Let us, then, adopt the Italian adage: "Don't pick mushrooms unless your grandfather did." Foraging is risky, not only because we don't always know what we are picking, but because we don't know who or what was there before; the picturesque idea of "wayside weeds" hardly bears scrutiny when you think about an *actual* wayside. By all means gather elderflowers and blackberries in fields, or ramps in woodland— if you are sure it *is* actually wild garlic you are picking—but, otherwise, forage in the gardens of friends (ask first!) or grow the kinds of things that you can forage in your own.

### Elderflowers and elderberries

Wild garlic, wood garlic, bear garlic, or ramps—these odoriferous wild flowers announce their presence by scent before you see them.

Elder has long been gathered in late spring for its blossom, which is easily made into a sweet cordial. But the blue-black immunity-boosting berries are just as showy in the fall and appear in time for cough and cold season. An elderberry syrup is warmly sweet, made with lemon, cloves, and cinnamon. Elderberry comes with a warning, though: the seeds, stems, leaves, and roots are toxic when raw (its toxicity disappears when cooked.)

# The science of taste

Taste has a close relationship with smell. Mouthwatering aromas are a prelude to foods that will taste good, since a person's sense of smell triggers anticipatory saliva as well as digestive juices. Scientists have given taste, in all its variety, just five flavor groups: sweet, salty, savory (or umami), sour, and bitter. Sweet is our base-line flavor at birth, and we learn to like the others. A baby will spit out bitter or sour food as a defense mechanism against poison, or food that is "off:" many poisons are bitter, and the bitterness of toxic plants was developed as a warning to herbivores.

Tolerance and enjoyment of different flavors comes not only from experience and social conditioning, but is also dependent on an individual's taste papillae—mainly on the sides, front, and back of the tongue—which house the taste buds. The great pleasure of food and its ultimate taste is a multisensory experience; flavor is tied up with the smell, texture, and temperature as well as the appearance of a meal.

As we have become more used to eating food that has traveled long distances (because it is out of season, or doesn't grow, where we live), so we have grown accustomed to a loss of nutrients in produce that we still consider fresh. Our abundance of choice has ironically led to a narrowing of diversity in food. People choose the same flavors all year round, even if that means woody asparagus and pale winter strawberries. In a garden, or in a landscape, variety in plants is essential, bringing with it many different beneficial insects and microbes, which in turn keep the soil in fine fettle. Our bodies—especially our gut microbiomes—are a bit like the soil, in that a food monoculture is inimical to the array of options that we need, weakening our immune defenses and opening doors to intolerances and allergies.

Asparagus is not sweet, sour, salty, or bitter: it is savory (umami). Other umami foods include potato, garlic, and tomato.

# How to enhance good tastes

Gluts are sometimes decorative, such as squashes and gourds stored in a porch or cool room, but they can also be put to efficient use. Repurposing a garage as an old-fashioned cold storage will rescue surpluses of apples and root vegetables. Dry pantries, still extant in some old houses, are cold rooms with a grate for a window; the space that is referenced hopefully on food packaging as "a cool, dark place." Fresh produce could be kept in the hall if that is cooler than the kitchen. Besides the ritual making of preserves, syrups, and vinegars, some fruits (such as raspberries and currants) can be kept in the freezer, to be revived months later. And don't forget the pleasantly useful line of pots on a windowsill in winter for basil, thyme, and mint.

### Making garden tastes last longer

If you consider the idea that homegrown peas need not be a one-off treat but can be grown for early, mid-, and late season cropping, and that lettuce can be picked all year, the idea of successional sowing is a good trade-off. As long as you have somewhere to sow seeds, with everything you need close at hand, it could become second nature; you may find that you have become a better gardener and eater, and also a better shopper. At a farmer's market you might pause over Casperita squash or Catalogna chicory not just because it looks fabulous, but because you could feasibly cook it (and the grower might explain how). At a French market, you'll grasp whether it is *herbes de Provence* (savory, marjoram, thyme, oregano) or *fines herbes* (parsley, chives, tarragon, chervil) that you need. In Italian markets they sell seeds and young plants as well as the fully ripe specimens, because people enjoy growing food with flavor.

Even if you don't consider yourself a fan of turnips, the vitality of the produce at a farmer's market could make you change your mind.

The expression *hors d'oeuvre* means "out of work," or in this case "outside of the meal," and it can be wonderful fun to take that literally. There is no "cheffing" involved in presenting a few small radishes, baby carrots, sliced cucumber (with its unrecognizable home-grown texture and taste), and a small bowl of sea salt flakes, or figs with Manchego cheese. Salad ingredients are also best when they haven't been pummeled with a strong dressing: a dish of sliced tomatoes benefits from the best olive oil, but it doesn't need anything else, except perhaps a scatter of salt at the last minute. Putting a dining table in your growing area is a way of embracing this kind of flavor-led approach to life; it's also a way of introducing it to your friends.

Heritage tomatoes come in many forms, but with their sun-ripened flavor they all say "high summer."

**"** If Eve had had a spade in Paradise and known what to do with it, we should not have had all that sad business of the apple. **"**

Elizabeth von Arnim, *Elizabeth and her German Garden*, 1898

# Plants for taste

### Raspberry  *Rubus idaeus*

Fall-ripening raspberries have the edge on their summer relations; they can't be bought. With a full flavor deepened over the entire summer, they don't need netting (birds are less interested this late in the season), and are therefore perfect for mobile eating. Try yellow raspberries for a bit more sweetness and added color. Harvest them after a meal when you're ready to eat them, for maximum freshness. Never tug a raspberry; there should be easy separation between fruit and cone.

**Prune old wood to the ground in February and mulch with heavy compost. Sun or semi-shade.**

### Sorrel  *Rumex acetosa*

Sorrel resembles a young, palatable dock leaf, with the oxalic acid hit of rhubarb, both of which it is related to. In northern Italy it is fondly called *pan e vino* (bread and wine), since the slightly chunky leaf, eaten while pruning olive trees, is filling as well as thirst-quenching. It has an intriguing taste: first bitter, then overwhelmingly vinegary. Young sorrel leaves go into a salad; older are cooked like spinach; either way, it's delicious and unusual.

**Prefers sun and good drainage.**

### Mint  *Mentha*

Mint is instantly soothing as tea: just pour boiling water onto a sprig. As an addition to cold drinks, it brings more depth of flavor than the word "garnish" would imply. There are many varieties: black peppermint is a handsome leaf, with a stronger flavor than its parent plant spearmint; fuzzy apple mint is invitingly tactile and translates well as a cooking ingredient. A hardy perennial, its roots like to run, in as large a space as possible. Keep trimming it and try to stop it from flowering, thus reducing its potency.

**Happy in semi-shade.**

### Cut-and-come-again lettuce

Cut-and-come-again lettuce leaves can be harvested all year round. On finding success with summer salad seed mixes, which are a pleasure to gather from a pot outside, you might want to grow more of the varieties that you like. Mustards add some heat to a bowl of sweeter lettuce, and tolerate cold weather, as Chinese mustard 'Green in Snow' implies. Non-heading lettuce leaves are harvested over weeks by picking around the base, the leaves soon regenerating.

**Moist soil, in semi-shade.**

Clockwise from top left: *Raspberry, Sorrel, Cut-and-come-again lettuce.*

> **"Pretty ground cover and an obliging disguiser of sharp edges, alpine strawberries are the ultimate unbuyable fruit"**

**Dandelion**  *Taraxacum*

Anyone curious to try a dandelion should feel free to do so; every part of it is edible. Young foliage gathered in early spring (before it becomes coarse and sour) is full of the vitamins and minerals that we all need after a long winter. Pleasantly bitter, mixing well with other salad greens, dandelion is a known diuretic and *aide-digestif*. Real dandelion enthusiasts grow it from seed, blanching the leaves as the season progresses, to keep them tender. Sliced at the base it looks exactly like curly endive; in fact, though a different genus, it's in the same overall family.

**Grows anywhere!**

**Tomato**  *Solanum lycopersicum*

A specimen from the refrigerator, possibly grown hydroponically, is a far cry from a warm, sun-ripened heritage tomato—the kind that says, in its flavor and juice, everything about the decadence and indulgence of a long, ripening summer. A greenhouse is useful, although reasonable results can be had by growing against a warm wall in cooler climates. The superior flavor and aroma means you should consider an unusual variety, such as 'Green Tiger', 'Black Plum', or 'Chianti Rose'.

**Pinch out the side shoots and keep it mulched, fed, and watered.**

**Alpine strawberry**  *Fragaria vesca*

With leaves, flowers, and fruits that make a pretty ground cover and an obliging disguiser of sharp edges, alpine strawberries are the ultimate unbuyable fruit. Added to breakfast or eaten as a snack, alpine strawberries are sweeter than candy, but, if you don't take the time to check that every side is red, the acidity is acute. They need to be eaten quickly before they lose their vitality and collapse.

**Grow in well-drained, fertile soil in sun or shade. They will soon spread around the garden on runners; thin them by pulling these off, along with smaller plants.**

From top to bottom *Dandelion, Tomato.*

**Cucumber**  *Cucumis sativus*

The flavor of a cucumber from the garden is so mellow, it is like eating sweetened air with a bit of salt. Home grown, the skin is softer and paler than those from the store, yet the flesh is crunchy. It is not watery, although the water content is 96 percent. Grow a heritage variety along with tomatoes— eat it with tomato too, in a gazpacho or a barely seasoned salad.

**Both heritage cucumbers and tomatoes benefit from the protection of a warm wall or greenhouse and plenty of organic matter.**

**Elderflower**  *Sambucus nigra*

A hedgerow weed, elderflower springs up with the enthusiasm of a sycamore but with palatable berries and blossom. The flowers make a refreshing cordial. Picked just after opening, its dessert-wine flavor translates into wine and champagne, while the cordial can help hay fever sufferers, especially if locally sourced (if they can get through the gathering process). Heavy with pollen, flower heads are easily foraged, but garden favorite *Sambucus nigra* f. *porphyrophylla* 'Eva' (a black form of elderflower) can also be used, pinkening a drink.

**Any aspect, any soil, sun, or partial shade.**

**Asparagus**  *Asparagus officinalis*

The taste and bite of (perfectly cooked) asparagus has the green notes of late spring and is an example of the flavor profile umami. The season is brief, and should be celebrated. Growing it is a longer-term garden proposition, with no harvesting for the first few years, followed by two decades of productivity. Female plants are ferny and berried, but the commonly grown male makes a strange sight, solitary spears rising from bare earth. Some suggest planting self-seeding parsley between rows as a ground cover and pollinator magnet.

**Fertile soil, cleared of perennial weeds.**

**Brussels sprout**  *Brassica oleracea* var. ***gemmifera***

Even buying Brussels sprouts on a stalk is less good than growing them, as they are already too old to eat. For a sprightly and uplifting flavor, aided by a slight crunch from steaming (never boiling), sprouts must be eaten immediately after picking. Brassicas are a molecule away from mustard gas and this is what you are moving toward when a sprout is old. For the best flavor, start picking (from the base) after the first frosts.

**They need very fertile soil and do best in a sunny, sheltered site.**

> **"**The finer points of its flavor have been overshadowed by its decorative value: bay doesn't enjoy being grown as a topiarized standard**"**

### Pea  *Pisum sativum*

The only peas that come close in flavor to homegrown varieties are frozen petite pois; the conversion of the latter's natural sugars into starch has been arrested at the right moment. It's important to pick garden peas when they are perfectly ripe for that fleeting pop of sweetness. Sow in succession and in quantity so that you can gather them by the bushel; they are moderately hardy and can be sown for harvesting in late spring and early summer, followed by the summer main crop—extending the season into the fall.

**Fertile soil, good drainage.**

### Bay  *Laurus nobilis*

Bay is worth more consideration than it normally gets on the way to a pot of stock or gravy. Once you notice the way it lifts a custard, preserve, or joint of meat, you will want to add more than one. Break a leaf to get a better grasp of the flavor, by experiencing the bay's aroma. The finer points of its flavor have been somewhat overshadowed by its decorative value: bay doesn't enjoy being grown as a topiarized standard by an exposed, north-facing front door.

**Try growing it free-range, in a sunny, sheltered, and well-drained spot.**

### Plum  *Prunus domestica*

A perfectly ripe plum seems to glow; catch it while the cool skin has a blush and the fruit is bursting with juice. There is a spectrum of flavor between the prized early damson and justly popular Victoria that supermarket "ripen at home" varieties can only dream of. A plum tree can be so abundant that the boughs hang down, ready to break. Keep on top of the glut by cooking and freezing them; clove, cinnamon, star anise, ginger, and wine lend themselves to their opulent flavor.

**Plum blossom comes in early spring and is vulnerable to frost; choose a sunny, sheltered site with fertile ground.**

Clockwise from top left *Pea, Bay, Plum.*

**Gooseberry**  *Ribes uva-crispa*

For maximum tartness, a semi-ripe gooseberry is preferable for some, and more useful in a pie or preserve. When fully ripened, the green or red globes can be eaten straight from the prickly bush, or frozen, or gently stewed. Their acidity demands to be made into a fool: balance gooseberry's piquancy with sweet elderflower syrup and heavy cream. Harvesting is easier on a standard plant, raising the spines off the ground; they grow well in containers.

**The most important considerations are sun, and plenty of water when the fruit's forming.**

**Nasturtium**  *Tropaeolum*

The fiery colors of nasturtium are a visual draw in the kitchen garden and also in a salad; after tossing it with dressing, add a few flowers, flower buds, or even young foliage. The peppery taste brings another layer of heat to oriental greens and is a good accent to milder leaves. Grow nasturtiums with fruit and vegetables; allow some to be sacrificed to blackfly aphids—thus luring them away from the green beans and providing a feast for ladybugs.

**Maximal light and the poorest, most sharply drained soil will lead to a good ratio of flowers over leaves in this half-hardy annual.**

**Beet**  *Beta vulgaris*

The leaves of beets are lovely to look at when they are growing happily in fertile soil, and are good to eat. Even people who don't like beets are sometimes drawn to beet soup, a dish that sees a transformation from earth dweller to a silky liquid of deepest magenta. In fact, very little needs to be added, besides cooking water, mustard, and balsamic vinegar.

**Can be grown all year; use the soil as storage space and earth up or cover with straw if they look ripe—only pull when ready.**

**Walnut**  *Juglans*

Walnuts are associated with winter, though their fresh nuts ripen in the fall. Remember that these are actually fruits, being "wet" with bite, rather than a soft crunch. Fresh nuts are excellent for eating in small quantities, before their green tea tannin overtones begin to dominate the nut flavor. They can be dried in a low-heat oven.

**The large and spreading walnut tree, in an old garden or perhaps or your own (if you can accommodate something that grows to 98ft/30 meters), is a handsome alternative to the beleaguered horse chestnut and should do well in soil that is moisture-retentive but well-drained.**

Clockwise from top *Nasturtium, Beet, Gooseberry.*

# SCENT

Scent can stop us in our tracks, take us back to precious times and places in our lives, or create new memories, in a way that no other sense can match. But it is as intangible as essential oils are volatile, and we are not all equally receptive to scent.

When a dog bounds outside, then pauses to sniff the air, it is clear that the sensation of smelling is among his greatest pleasures in life. It would be alarming for a person to be quite as smell-receptive, since a dog's nose is hyper-alert to every kind of aroma and odor, and, anyway, many of the scents he finds most fascinating would be frankly repellent to us. But there are many ways to create a garden that suits your nose perfectly.

Fragrance on fragrance:
opulent colors mix with
intense aromas when roses
are grown with honeysuckle.

# Ideas on a scented garden

Breathing deeply from a doorway or window is a good position to adopt, and not just on a sunny morning. It makes sense, then, to "edit" the smells around a garden entrance to be pleasing, aiming not just for an occasional waft, but for a more tangible hit of fragrance that can be taken in deep breaths, drawing you further outside.

## Surrounded by scent

Sometimes, the scents that stop you in your tracks come from unexpected sources. Skimmia is a useful but undramatic evergreen shrub which looks its worst in early spring, just as it is preparing to explode into panicles of warm, pale flowers that pull in the March bees and pump out month-long scent. Where is that radiant vanilla fragrance coming from? you might ask every year, before remembering the diffident shrub by the front door. Other stalwart evergreens such as daphne, mahonia, and varieties of *Viburnum* x *bodnantense* bring earlier cheer, as they are winter-flowering, but scent is volatile and is subject to weather and light levels, as well as to a person's olfactory receptors. It can be maddeningly elusive.

The opened-cologne-bottle of a bluebell wood needs to be experienced for us to grasp the maximum impact of plant fragrance. It's not only the mix of perfume and oxygen that makes you stand in awe in one of these woodlands, but the uninterrupted view of green, overlaid with a supernatural purple-blue, and a magical feeling of stillness. Saplings may be in fresh leaf, but if the bluebells are in a beech wood (and that's the ideal), the canopy that is still unfurling its leaves gives the plants the light that they need for flowering, followed by the shade they will require later in the season.

Daphnes are appreciated for wafting spicy scent through the winter air from small pink and white flowers. *Daphne odora* 'Aureomarginata' is a handsome evergreen.

Bluebells do best as a monoculture in a sheltered place; grown by the thousand, ethereal-looking *Hyacinthoides non-scripta* becomes more obviously related to its powerfully scented cousin, the hyacinth. Single bluebells, lovely though they are in grass, are easily overlooked.

Ethereal bluebells, grown in quantity, release their magical scent.

### Fragrance and memory

It is telling that there seem to be more descriptions of bad smells than of good, with tautologies tumbling over one another to describe a putrid stink, malodorous stench, or reeking effluvium. The words are revealingly arcane: life was more vividly smelly in the past, when people kept posies within easy reach of their noses—held, or tied to a wrist, pinned on a hat, secured behind the ear, or worn as a corsage. Sweet violet and lily-of-the-valley, usefully small with a powerful scent, now look distinctly Victorian, although in the perfume industry their individual scents have always had currency. Garden fragrances are beyond fashion, even if a plant's appearance is tied to past associations. Ionone, the essence of violet scent, has been made synthetically for more than a century, while violet and lily-of-the-valley aromas both persist in modern perfume.

Of all the senses, it is smell that is the memory-trigger. Sometimes fond remembrances get mixed up with cultural overlays, and then we no longer know what to think of certain plants: Granny's lavender was wonderful to touch as a child, the smell divine, but now it can't shake off its old lady image. Silver-leafed aromatics—including the pungent curry plant and sharp artemisia—were all the rage in 1980s herb gardens, but are less easy to place within, say, the grassy perennial movement. So choose to move away from ideas of horticultural fashion; instead, consider your garden as an opportunity to develop a bouquet of the kind of aromas that you want to have around you.

### Create a "scent trap"

The ideal conditions for plants to release their molecules of fragrance include warmth, stillness, and humidity. In northern climes, we can go some way toward quieting the air by creating an enclosure (surrounded by windbreaks on a larger property) and then never letting a south- or west-facing wall go to waste. Brick absorbs heat during the day, releasing it slowly after sundown, which enables the success of more tender plants, such as stauntonia vine, star jasmine (*Trachelospermum jasminoides*), and a fruit for at least four of the senses: fig.

You might consider making a garden within a garden, with scented wisteria, climbing and shrub roses, garden pinks, peonies, and phlox.

Exotic plants such as angel's trumpets (which are poisonous) could be grown in large pots and stored over winter, to be positioned in the part of your garden where you spend summer evenings. Locate a sun trap and think of it as a scent trap, too: filled with fragrance that compels you to linger. Scents hold your attention, precluding rushing around.

Scent most commonly occurs in paler plants, hinting at their role for nocturnal pollinators. At dusk, honeysuckle, night-scented stock, and the freakishly beautiful tobacco plant *Nicotiana sylvestris* begin to send out potent wafts that could be described as a fragrance that is by turns fruity-floral, cloved, and headily spiced.

Having attracted hoverflies and bees to their pollen-heavy anthers during the day, lilies now pull in the night-pollinating moths, aided by a more powerful scent and their glowing, pale flowers. In warmth, *Lilium regale*, common jasmine, and varieties of lilac can be intoxicating... and are sometimes overpowering. They share the scent compound indole, in which a slightly animalic whiff becomes stronger as a plant ages, and can smell positively sickly to some people. Lilies grow well in pots, which can be convenient if they need to be wheeled further away. As the American literary figure Katherine White observed, "One gardener's perfume is another gardener's stink."

The resin of woody plants makes a stirring base note for a fragrance: think of a stand of pine trees by the beach, or pencil cypress in southern Europe. Aromatics such as rosemary and lavender are woody too, and combine well in a garden. Every part of these plants, as well as those of pelargonium contain essential oils, which are the "attar" or essence of a plant's taste and smell.

Scented pelargoniums are very tactile, their fuzzy, distinctive leaves releasing essential oils when rubbed. The spectrum is wide, with flowers often intensely hued.

Rubbing the leaves will give you more than enough information on which to base your preferences, and, with pelargoniums, there is a myriad of varieties to choose from. A small greenhouse or conservatory filled with them will give you the most fabulous velvet colors, and, in the varieties where leaf shape, texture, and fragrance are more arresting than the flower, an attar of lemon, mint, apple, or the classic, eponymous *Pelargonium* 'Attar of Roses'.

**Grow-your-own aromatherapy**

If you are open to the kind of therapies that are there in the garden for the taking, you could rub rosemary for memory (medical science backs Ophelia on this: studies have shown that rosemary triggers memory). The early blue flowers also provide important nectar for emerging bees. Lavender is perhaps the best-selling essential oil in the world and is regarded, in nonmedical parlance, as a cure-all: helping to neutralize headaches, and, unarguably, enhancing mood. An oil diffuser indoors is one way of becoming familiar with the world of essential oils, not all of which are easily grown or found, but a garden interim would be a pot of tender French lavender (*Lavandula stoechas*), the fuzzy rabbit-eared variety that just asks to be stroked. Harvest the flowers of regular lavender as they begin to open.

Essential oils are produced in the leaves of mint and lemon verbena, as well as black currant. The deep and warm aroma of lemon verbena (folk name: "magic wort") is easily released by rubbing the leaves; keep it near where you sit in the sun. Put simply, it makes you feel good. Even at Sissinghurst, the garden created by Vita Sackville-West, a pot of lemon verbena was kept by a chair outside the castle

Lavender releases essential oils when you brush past. Harvest it for drying early, just after the dew evaporates, when just under half is in flower.

cottage, so that the occupants could rub its leaves while reading, years before anyone brought the words "aroma therapy" into general conversation and tied them together.

Citrus contains essential oils in its peel; a more potent drink than hot water and lemon juice is hot water with strips of lemon zest; you will not look back. Similarly, the zests of lemon and orange used in cooking add another dimension of aroma—and therefore taste—than simply adding the juice. In the perfume industry, scent is drawn from many sources, but plants are the main providers of floral fragrance. And yet, perfume is only an interpretation of a natural smell. So, when smelling roses, be generous with your time; a good whiff is more memorable than a spritz of *parfum*. If lilac strikes a primal chord, and it doesn't with everybody, bury your face in the silky, opulent blooms. Or try night-scented stock: it would be impossible to get such a pleasurable hit from a dried clove.

Beauty in waste: a healthy, vital compost heap has no noticeable odor, but the value of the finished product is evident in its looks, feel, and smell.

# Compost

If someone proudly offers their home-made compost for you to sniff, the concept may seem bizarre. Yet finished compost is known as "black gold" due to its benefits—it smells valuable too: deep, earthy, full of vitality. It is garden waste, slowly transformed into a nutritious garden "blanket" with the aid of microbes, moisture, and oxygen. The smell of humus on a forest floor is more complex, as it includes more pronounced odors from animal decay and fungi, lifted by the life-giving aroma of leaves photosynthesizing.

It is the odor of anaerobic decomposition that people dislike: a lack of oxygen leads to the fetid smell of stagnation, or methane. Compost "tea" is notorious because the age-old approach of putting mineral-rich plant material into a bucket with water and jamming on a lid can result in an unpleasant smell. It is called leachate, and it has its benefits, but aerated "tea" is preferable and smells as good as aerated compost. A fairly straightforward approach to feeding the soil is to make your own compost and enrich it by adding leaves rich in potassium (such as comfrey, ideally the 'Bocking 14' variety) and nitrogen (nettles). It's a good way of disposing of weeds, while turning compost is good exercise, and it's aerobic.

### Stinky fungi

Stinkhorn is the most famously malodorous fungus, with looks that are difficult to ignore: the species is called *Phallus*, which is a clue to its appearance. Its smell, a mixture of rotting meat and feces, is heavenly for flies, which it needs to attract for dispersing its spores. Fungi in all their huge variety are absolutely crucial in breaking down the decaying matter of the earth. Without them, the world would be intolerably smelly.

# The science of scent

Cut grass is a well-loved smell, but why? Some people say it is the scent of summer, with countryside overtones. It can bring back childhood memories, of a household's grown-ups mowing the lawn—the fragrance of comforting order and routine. Others might prefer the drier, sweeter notes of hay. When something "smells", it is the result of the olfactory sensory neurons, high up in the nose, being stimulated by tiny odor molecules which—in the case of cut grass—are carbon-based compounds called green leaf volatiles. Plants frequently send them out in response to damage, and with mowing, the volatiles are more concentrated, delivering a stronger signal to the olfactory bulb in the brain.

From here, olfactory signals move straight to the limbic system, where the amygdala at the base of the brain, and the hippocampus behind it, process emotional response as well as the making and storing of memories. Up until adolescence, smell (along with touch) is a person's most developed sense, having already begun to form in the womb. The scents you experience at a young age, therefore, are closely linked with your early experience. Not all smell memories are equal; sometimes a certain aroma triggers a particularly powerful response—and there it is, a Proustian moment.

We have different levels of sensitivity to scent, with unequal chemical and emotional responses. Our sense of smell also diminishes with age. It is possible to improve olfactory responses, however, by exercising the smell sense like a muscle, through consciously sniffing and identifying the varying components of what you are smelling. The plain fact that the not-unpleasant fragrance of freshly cut grass is really the smell of plant trauma is, unfortunately for the grass, irrelevant.

For people, a freshly mown path or lawn smells of the joys of summer; for grass, it's another matter.

# How to strengthen scent in your garden

When planning for scent, think vertically and aerially, while raising smaller plants off the ground, so they will be closer to nose height.

**Creating a scented garden**

Rambling roses and pergolas go well together; if you are prepared to put up with a slightly unruly tunnel, you will gain a hit of pure rose scent (and sparrows and other small birds love this unmanicured tangle). Other scented pergola favorites are *Clematis armandii* and honeysuckle (again, not so tidy), gently fragranced passionflower, and chocolate-smelling *Akebia quinata. Viola odorata* in white, pink, or violet is exquisite to look at as well as to inhale and it would do well in a trough or at the edge of a retaining wall.

Hedges are another option for moving scent closer to us. There are many roses that can be planted in quantity to form a hedge and *Rosa rugosa* is a popular parking lot plant for a reason (it also thrives near beaches). Rugosas are reliable and tough, but so much more, being very floriferous, with healthy, attractively creased leaves and a sedating scent. They are not all magenta: perhaps choose pale pink *Rosa* 'Fru Dagmar Hastrup', or white 'Blanche Double de Coubert'. They have lustrous red hips in the fall.

In the landscape, it is worth looking for linden (lime) trees, and standing under one when it is in flower. The light, bright honeyed aroma is a surprise, emanating from such a seemingly green tree, until you know that linden flower has for centuries been an important ingredient in perfumery. Better still, if a lime tree can smell this good, the chances are that it will attract bees: linden is a loud, buzzing tree for a few weeks in June.

Tumbling, rambling roses such as 'Paul's Himalayan Musk' dispense fragrance aerially, hanging from trees and structures. Rambling roses need minimal pruning.

## Bringing the outside in

One way of enjoying some winter scent is by bringing a flowering branch into the house and putting it into a vase with water. Cutting a branch is not very significant for a tree and counts as a light pruning. You can also cut woody winter flowers to hold their scent captive, such as elegant evergreen *Sarcococca confusa*, with its small white ribbon petals as well as black shiny berries, while pink-flowered *Viburnum* x *bodnantense* smells expensive in a small room. Mahonia's slightly prehistoric appearance is dramatically altered by separating a sulphur-yellow flower from its jagged leaves and making a specimen of it: the focus is on the scent. Fruit blossoms bring a lift into a home; later, quince fruit fills a room with heavenly, yellow-floral fragrance.

In warmer weather, pick flowers for cutting early in the day, with a bucket or vase filled with water close at hand. Besides holding back the volatile fragrances, you will want to immerse yourself in the slow ritual of sizing up and cutting, with a chorus of birds and insects adding to the early-morning magic. The classics of scent are blousy and romantic, not necessarily emanating from show-garden flowers. Think of old-fashioned philadelphus, phlox, cottage pinks, and nectar-rich jonquils in spring. Grow them in profusion in an unregimented cutting garden. Don't worry about grouping the scents: mix them up for a living fragrance bouquet, the envy of any perfumer.

The powerful scent of *Sarcococca* makes itself known through the gloom of winter but bringing in a sprig of *S. hookeriana* var. *digyna* makes an easy, fragrant display indoors.

**"** The rose looks
fair, but fairer
we it deem
For that sweet
odor which doth
in it live. **"**

**William Shakespeare,** *Sonnet 54*, **1609**

# Plants for scent

### Rose  *Rosa*

What is a rose without scent? Lovely, yes, but if you grow just one rose it has to be scented. And maybe repeat-flowering. Catalogs are sumptuous but complicated: perhaps narrow your choice to an old or English shrub rose, or a climber you can train on a wall. Covering a pergola with a fragrant rambler involves very little pruning, its unruly tangle of blossoms hanging down to form a scent enclosure.

**Roses are easy to care for, preferring a heavier, weed-free soil. They do best in sun.**

### Honeysuckle  *Lonicera*

Delightful in a hedgerow, a honeysuckle in your own hedge will make it look less neat but more enchanting, and preferable to the bird's nest effect when the plant is grown against a column or wall. Honeysuckle responds well to a hard prune; when the tendrils are young it's easy to loosely tie them onto railings or a fence so that they are not waving in the sky. The colors of Dutch and American honeysuckle are as divine as the evening scent; white and yellow *Lonicera periclymenum* 'Graham Thomas' is super-reliable.

**They grow toward the sun, preferring shade at the base.**

### Lily  *Lilium*

A pot of lilies can turn a terrace or courtyard into a garden, with their stately progression from foliage, to swelling pelican-beak bud, to the curled-back petals of a painting from an Italian church. It's all there with easy-to-grow *Lilium regale*. Pollen-heavy anthers attract every kind of pollinator, and, in the evening, the blooms take on the appearance of trumpets, blasting out an exotic, heavy scent. In the ground, tall, freckled-orange *L. henryi* is a spicy turk's cap lily, which prefers wet feet.

**Lilies are happy in semi-shade.**

### Lilac  *Syringa*

If the musky, nostalgic scent of lilac sends you into raptures, you will accept that its exceptional fragrance outweighs its ineffectual appearance for the rest of the year. You will also ignore the old wives' tale that lilac shouldn't be cut and brought indoors. Its foppish habit, like a curled 17th-century wig, looks even better in a vase, ideally next to your bed for heady, floral dreams. Remove leaves and sear the stems in boiling water for 30 seconds, to prevent drooping. Seek out the more showy varieties, to get you in the mood for summer.

**Full sun.**

Clockwise from top left  *Lilac, Lily, Honeysuckle.*

> **"The allium odor of *Nectaroscordum siculum* makes itself known as you brush past: a rank, garlicky mustard"**

### Stock  *Matthiola*

Night-scented stock comes in many varieties, from pretty but spindly *Matthiola longipetala* (such as pale lilac 'Starlight Scentsation'), to the florist's choice, stout and multibloomed *Matthiola incana* (warm pink 'Aida Apricot'). Either way, the scent is like catnip for humans if you like the smell of cloves in the evening. They are nectar- and pollen-rich, attracting bees, butterflies, and moths.

**Stocks need moisture at their feet, full sun, and shelter. Grow the smaller varieties massed, for more impact.**

### Sicilian honey garlic
*Nectaroscordum siculum*

Generally known as nectaroscordum, its looks alone make it worthwhile: an ornamental onion that is intriguing and lovely at every stage, from drooping bells of plaster-pink and verdigris to arrowed seed heads that reach upward like a vertical bonnet. The allium odor makes itself known as you brush past: a rank, garlicky mustard. In a garden's sweet bouquet, it adds a steadying note amid all those "prettier" scents.

**A self-seeder, it needs full sun to stop it from flopping around.**

### Katsura tree  *Cercidiphyllum japonicum*

On still fall days, the Katsura tree responds to a sunny spell with a distinct aroma of cooking sugar. Once you catch the surprising scent, for some it can disappear again like the Cheshire cat, while others might smell it strongly. Having drawn attention to itself for the first time since spring, Katsura's heart-shaped leaves are enjoyably autumnal in mainly deep yellow or shades of pink.

**A tall, fairly slender, and conical tree (reaching about 26ft/8m in 20 years), it is a good proposition in a walled or sheltered woodland garden.**

Left *Sicilian honey garlic.*

**Mahonia**  *Mahonia aquifolium*

Mahonias deserve better than the uninviting corners to which they are so often relegated. There are some real stars among the *lamariifolia* and *media* species, the latter smelling like lily-of-the-valley in early winter. It appreciates some sun, so put it somewhere more prominent where you might stop and notice it, even thinning out the branches of *M. x media* and pruning it to eye and nose height, to make a better show of its dinosaur leaves and glow-in-the-dark yellow flowers.

Hardy evergreen.

**Lemon verbena**  *Aloysia citrodora*

The energizing citrus of lemon verbena is appreciated in France (and easily available as vervain tea bags). Yet elsewhere the herb is still something of a secret. Like mint, its essential oils are instantly comforting: as well as harvesting leaves for a tea, the deep and warm aroma is easily released by rubbing the leaves now and again. Keep this self-effacing plant within constant view, as a reminder for lifting the spirits.

Not hardy; brought indoors it looks positively dead in winter, but with sunlight, watering, and some pruning it slowly comes back to life.

**Curry plant**  *Helichrysum italicum*

Aromatics come alive in the heat; the hotter they get, the more they radiate their essential oils. These can be pungent, although the curry plant has nothing to do with Asian spices. Happy in gravel, or near hot paving, it needs no shade whatsoever. It's the silvery leaves that appeal to gardeners, bouncing light around an enclosed space. Mixed with other drought-tolerant plants such as thyme and artemisia, the variety of smells draws in beneficial insects.

Woody perennial; small aromatic branches are added to Mediterranean stews.

**Garden pink**  *Dianthus*

Dianthus, or pinks, or gillyflowers (literally meaning "clove-scented") are delightfully cottagey, and join the evening-scented tribe, having attracted beneficial insects all day. Pinks like to bake in the sun, their pointed, silvery leaves forming mats along a path edge. Mixing well with herbs, pinks are also happy in a rose garden. They have appeared in paintings of flowery meads from the early Renaissance; the best have dowdy names such as 'Mrs. Sinkins' and 'Gran's Favorite' (far right).

Short-lived, yet easily replaceable by taking cuttings.

Clockwise from top *Mahonia, Garden pink, Lemon verbena.*

> **"Keep *Nicotiana sylvestris* where it can be appreciated in the gloaming, sending out wafts of spicy, exotic fragrance"**

Clockwise from top left *Flowering tobacco, Sweet pea, French marigold.*

### Flowering tobacco *Nicotiana sylvestris*

The tobacco plant looks as decadent as it smells (with no obvious connection to the aroma of dried tobacco). Smaller tobacco plants are container favorites, but statuesque *Nicotiana sylvestris* is the most dramatic. Its drooping white trumpets are balanced by wide, bright green, sticky, toxic leaves; keep it somewhere sheltered so that it doesn't keel over in the wind and where it can be appreciated in the gloaming, sending out wafts of spicy, exotic fragrance.

Half-hardy annual; keep young plants in pots, away from slugs until they are tougher. Sun or semi-shade; moist but well-drained soil.

### Sweet pea *Lathyrus odoratus*

Sweet peas have a treasured place in the annals of scent nostalgia, a close runner-up to roses. These hardy annuals belong in kitchen gardens, cutting gardens, by the back door, or anywhere you can get to them easily for the frequent cutting they need to keep flower production going. Old-fashioned *Lathyrus odoratus* is the most deeply (and spicily) scented, especially in the oldest varieties, 'Matucana' and 'Cupani', introduced in the 1690s.

Sow in the fall and early spring for an extended season, constructing a sizable wigwam before planting.

### French marigold *Tagetes patula*

Certain varieties are so magnificent in their richly colored velvet, with names to match ('Cinnabar', 'Linnaeus Burning Embers') that it's hard to believe they are marigolds. In handling them, however, memories are sharply revived of the old-fashioned kind of spick-and-span border, free from any signs of life except a row of highly pungent orange or yellow marigolds, squatting in the midday sun. Banish such reminiscences by growing leggy *Tagetes* in pots or near tomatoes.

Full sun and moisture. They are malodorous to white fly.

**Thyme**  *Thymus*

A life-enhancing aromatic. Lightly roasted, its scent recalls the sustained sunshine that it requires—the longer and hotter the better. A low-growing woody evergreen shrub, common or lemon thymes are the best for cooking, although their flowery, variegated relations make good neighbors. The dark red flowers of creeping thyme form a quietly spectacular ground cover and an effective edging over a ledge, or reaching across paving.

Grow it in a site that's open, light, and bright; with sharp drainage and untilled soil.

**Garden phlox**  *Phlox paniculata*

The smells of North American woodland are sweetened by peppery wild phlox, the ancestor to the English flower border favorites. It is natural that phlox should require semi-shade and moist, humus-rich soil, and, when denied it, the plants are prone to mildew. The range of shades in the different cultivars are rich, traveling through the color wheel from blue to all kinds of pink and purple, and they still send out scent long after dark despite their darker hues. *P. paniculata* 'David' is the showy white one.

Herbaceous perennial.

**Mock orange**  *Philadelphus coronarius*

A wonderfully blowsy shrub with an orange-blossom and jasmine aroma, which partly explains its common name (it also slightly resembles orange blossom). A mid-century favorite ripe for revival, it goes into the "romantic" category, perhaps as part of a cutting garden of aroma, texture, and high days of undisciplined beauty. Like lilac, it reverts to inconspicuous shrub status when not in flower in June. Cultivars 'Belle Etoile', 'Manteau d'Hermine', and 'Sybille' are best for looks and scent.

Sun or semi-shade.

**Angels trumpet**  *Brugmansia*

Tender greenhouse flowers, brought out in summer. Perhaps because they come with the warning "all parts are toxic" they have a narcotic quality, enhanced by their dramatically draped South American blooms, like a dancer's dress in *Flying Down to Rio*. The aroma is gloriously, fruitily tropical. This is an adults-only plant and the magnetic blooms should be kept out of the path of children and animals. Buds are spiraled like a closed umbrella; the blooms can be pale apricot, subtle yellow, or pink, and "moonflower" white.

Frequent watering.

Right *Mock orange.*

# SIGHT

The proverb "beauty is in the eye of the beholder" was never truer than in a garden. For some people, creating a garden view becomes a list of chores; it can never reach its potential because it will never be finished. For others, there is beauty in the process: every stage of every season—and each new project accomplished—bringing something to delight in. Then there are those who are mainly interested in crisp edges and definite form, the absence of which in an outdoor space means that they don't feel they are looking at a garden at all, but at a wilderness.

A garden can be as simple as a few plants of purple, white, and green, with lupins, alliums, and honesty. The latter two have excellent seed heads to keep it all going when the flowers are over.

# Ideas on sight, views, and beauty

A good framework for your garden needs to be a priority. It will mean that, within this structural place, you'll be able to zoom in on the details you create, without worrying about the general imperfections, or jobs left undone. Design is something you can do yourself, when you think about a back garden or an urban front area in terms of heights and volumes. In other words, you need to consider hard landscaping for getting around, and then some trees and shrubs both to create this height and volume and for hiding things that you don't want in view.

### Own your view

There will be things in your view that don't belong to you, and which you'd rather not focus on every time you look out of the window. This can be remedied not with an enormous evergreen hedge, but a kind of horticultural net curtain. Plants on the windowsill do make a difference, but, better still, plant a climbing Madame Alfred Carrière rose under the kitchen window: it will spread around both sides while framing your view, and, given a sunny position, it will do the same for the window above. As soon as you have a rose by the house, you will have life, with pollinators and birds.

### Garden visitors

Birds are an enchanting diversion, but they are not interested in a solitary decorative bird bath in the middle of a lawn. Smaller birds need cover nearby. Roses around the window are a wonderful lure, especially when you add a transparent feeder, attached to the window on suction cups. They will then have somewhere to perch while considering whether to venture to the feeder, and, when sparrows get the hang of it,

The space between a townhouse and the street is an opportunity: here, grasses provide movement and a focus for flowers.

they'll soon be pecking aphids off your rose buds as well. Plants in the middle ground are also effective in creating a positive focus. Grasses move in the gentlest breeze and they make a good foil for long-stemmed plants, such as *Dianthus carthusianorum*. Trees with light canopies, such as birch, are also very effective as distraction, and not just around the edges; plant trees in the middle, too, creating lots of foreground to blur the background.

Seeing visitors enjoy your garden will put a positive perspective on it; even better when they are animals. Something as simple as a wide, shallow bowl near shrubs will attract hedgehogs as well as birds and beneficial insects. Or plant a bigger trough higher off the ground for the purpose of staring at water lilies, and install a very gentle pump to deter breeding mosquitoes but not the birds.

Water is mesmerizing, like fire. The two can be combined, with candles in jars and larger storm lanterns. In winter, lighting up the space outside a window is another opportunity for gazing, letting the mind wander, and for lighting up the exterior bleakness of a late January evening.

## Lighting the scene

Plants need light more than they need water, and people too are not generally drawn to spending time in the drab confines of an overshadowed garden. A knee-jerk reaction to lack of light is to start campaigning to get a tree cut down, when it might just need thinning. A sturdy trellis does not need to be swamped by *Clematis montana* (whose pruning regime is easily forgotten); a semitransparent barrier allows in light while distracting from neighbors even when it's barely covered. If no one is looking into your garden except for the odd dog or distant vehicle, keep its perimeter low. Light changes with the seasons: in the fall, the sun's sloping rays can look startlingly cinematic, highlighting trees that are already changing color. When this happens, rush out and enjoy it, like a dramatic sunset. If your grasses are not backlit at this time of year, move them to a position where they are.

## A landscape in a garden

When you start to look, you see more. If you live in the country or within reach of a large park, shrubs and trees offer up a feast of minute detail, with every season highlighting something which is more prevalent than it was in the previous year. In the fall, it might be dark red berries in a hedge of coloring leaves—perhaps it's a good year for berries, or maybe it's the first time you've noticed this type.

Blossom meets in the middle when cow parsley reaches up toward fruit trees in spring.

There is so much blossoming in spring, in a long progression, that there is enough time to witness the changes. From flowering thorns—beginning with blackthorn, alive with bees in March—to further white flower clusters on wild plums and cherries, followed by froths of white on the long stems of cow parsley everywhere. You will discover that learning the names of plants in the landscape also opens the eyes.

Beginning with snowdrops and winter aconite, the wildflowers of spring in northern climes pull the eyes down: primroses and cowslips are easy to identify, but, a few weeks later, you might start to take note of the wayside weeds, too. Their folk names will of course be unique to where you live, but always reveal the plant's cherished position in the past, mainly for curing aches and pains. You might find Jack-in-the-hedge, herb Robert, self-heal, hairy bitter cress—the latter an easily overlooked little weed which horticulturalist Gertrude Jekyll recommended serving on toast.

Noticing local wildflowers can help in identifying the kinds of plants that might do well in your garden, with inspiring combinations drawn from nature. In June, fertile verges say everything about harmony in growing conditions: take luminous blue-violet meadow cranesbill—actually wild geraniums—mingling in grass with taller, creamy-topped meadowsweet. In a garden, meadowsweet will spread when happy, but that's no reason not to buy it—and keep it in check. As for hardy geraniums, they are surely in the pantheon of most-useful plants; G. 'Brookside' is a good color match with the wild version. Devil's bit scabious is a heavenly pincushion flower, despite its name. When placing scrambling scabious in a garden, memories of palest purple-blue dotting a field of wildflowers is a good mental image to reference.

The wildflower known as Devil's bit scabious (*Succisa pratensis*) makes an instant garden and a perfect color combination just by mingling with meadow grass.

## The art of gazing

If you start to really look and appreciate the details of summer, you'll find that you see a lot more in winter, too. The colder months are the most useful time for gazing out of the window, when the structure of your outdoor space is laid bare. Look at shapes and silhouettes: does a tree need all that ivy, blurring its lines? Can you put shrubs somewhere else, instead of crowding another tree? Time to order more snowdrops. Winter's visual highlights are in the outlines: bare branches of oak, looking like inverted tree roots; the quality of a wall; newly revealed birds' nests, built in surprising places. On the morning of a frost, get outside— when the leaves of dark evergreens are traced in every detail, and crystalline spiders' webs give some insight into the importance of a hedge for habitat.

Winter is an underrated season, but its splendors shouldn't be missed. Witch hazel, a shrub or small tree, needs a little space around it, and some backlighting from the low, winter sun—ready for its deep-winter inflorescence. Ribbonlike flowers, often scented, reach out of the gloom in the richest warm colors, instead of the chilly pinks and mauves of many scenters of the winter air. For outstanding elegance, hellebore competes with any summer flower, and is a superior item for months at a time at the end of winter, seeing out the comings and goings of snowdrops and crocus. *Crocus tommasinianus* (the small type that naturalizes in lawns) is another early flower, with a serious bolt of color in ringing violet-purple with orange anthers; the kind of tonal combination that you hadn't realized that you'd missed until now, broadcasting news of spring all over the grass.

Crocus is one of the best sights in spring, partly because of the intense and luminous color combinations. They look perfect in tired old grass, among the odd dead leaf and fallen twig.

If you have room for one tree, let it be crab apple. It will give you something to look at for most of the year, while bringing in the noises of nature, scent, tactility—and it may even stir you into making jelly.

### Perfection in a plant

Some plants give meaning to the garden center legend, "long season of interest;" they are genuinely interesting, and have peak moments over at least two seasons. Crab apple is an amazing all-arounder, having pretty blossom that is often pink and white simultaneously (and far removed from some ornamental cherry pinks, which can be difficult to place). Crab apples are among the best trees for insects and birds; in *Malus* x *robusta* 'Red Siberian', clusters of sour scarlet fruits remain on the tree well into winter. It's engrossing to watch blackbirds clinging on and eating them, and, later, cardinals, cedar waxwings, and robins come in from the frozen fields to finish them off. Crab apples with orange and ocher fruit glow in early winter against bare branches, along with the berries of European mountain ash trees—another favorite with birds.

There are plants that do everything that is promised, with wonderful leaves, good proportions, and a beautiful buildup, followed by months of flower color, which only gets more interesting as they age. These include the enormous range of hydrangeas and euphorbias. Taller plant architecture comes from angelica, cardoon, and giant fennel, making a highly textural group. Giant scabious (*Cephalaria gigantea*) can also be counted here, with its summer screen of pale yellow flowers on long, branched stems over mounds of attractive leaves. Self-seeding poppies provide textural greenery with glaucous seed heads, but, at their best, the flowers of these annuals are outrageously visual in the pink-purple spectrum, sometimes mutating through cross-pollination into double-flowered pompoms. Perennial oriental poppies, along with bearded iris, are firecracker plants—supported by excellent, structural foliage.

The slow decay of a flower can be as enjoyable to watch as its development, which is certainly the case with tulips when cut and brought indoors. Every day, a homegrown, unsprayed tulip takes on a new persona, reacting to both the light and the slow draining of its life force. This is particularly dramatic with the ruffled "parrot" varieties. In a cooler room it is a show that can go on for two weeks. Roses, too, change daily: deep pink *Rosa* 'Gertrude Jekyll' metamorphoses from elegantly furled, to open-yet-pristine, to over-blowsy chintz, all within a day or two.

# Pollinators

"Nuisance" insects take on a new sheen when we know they aid pollination. Even bluebottle flies, with the thought-provoking Latin name of *Calliphora vomitoria*, are helpful (mainly in eating decaying matter). Wasps are pollen-eaters and therefore pollinators, spreading particles as they move. They are attracted to umbellifer plants, such as fennel and angelica, making a striking picture when they congregate in summer on the purple umbels of statuesque *Angelica gigas*.

More obviously pretty pollinators include the lacewing: almost transparent, with long gossamer wings over a slender neon-green body. Lacewing larvae are terrific aphid-eaters, as are those of the hoverfly. A hoverfly looks like a bee in aviator goggles, hovering intently next to pollinator-friendly plants.

Beetles were the first pollinators; magnolias evolved to attract them before bees even existed. Plants and pollinators have evolved together: the proboscises of moths—sometimes longer than their bodies—are designed for plunging into tubular flowers, without ever needing to land (flowers for butterflies have evolved with landing pads). Bats pollinate agave and banana flowers; hummingbirds hover, mothlike, at funnel-shaped flowers, using their beak like a proboscis.

Hoverflies—looking like bees in aviator goggles—are both prolific pollinators and lovely to watch in the garden.

### Making friends with larvae

Ladybugs help pollinate flowers, but are most interested in aphids; it is macabre fun, watching a ladybug lumber up to a plump greenfly and pick it up, legs flailing. When you see aphids, find a ladybug and bring it over. Once predator numbers rise during the summer, aphid problems will decrease. Ladybug larvae, looking like mini alligators, eat their weight in aphids every day, and thousands more as adults, so it is vital to recognize them as larva (see page 13) and pupa.

# The science of sight

Animal vision depends on photoreceptors—specialized light-sensitive cells in the eyes. The eyesight of humans is highly reliant on light and is poor in darker situations. Owls, being nocturnal predators, are equipped to see well in the dark—partly due to "eyeshine," in which their photoreceptors receive more light due to a reflecting layer behind the retina. In most animals, vision is connected with the hunt for food.

The visual dialogue between a nectar-producing flower and a butterfly is also invisible to humans; it's about the butterfly's survival, not ours. Most pollinators (insects, birds, the majority of bats) are equipped with ultraviolet vision. Butterflies can see flower markings containing pigments that are especially absorbent to ultraviolet light, often forming a bullseye at the nectar collection point, along with patterning on petals that can tell them where to land.

The lens of a human eye blocks ultraviolet light. When we look at common evening primrose, we see a bowl-shaped, solid yellow flower, but with the aid of ultraviolet light, it looks more like a garden pink or sweet William, with pale petals and a darker, rayed, eye. For bees, the equivalent of RGB (red, green, and blue, on which the color spectrum for humans is based) is ultraviolet light, green, and blue. They do not register red at all—although this is an important color for butterflies and pollinating birds. Colors that are most attractive to bees are blue, violet, purple, white, and yellow.

Compound eyes are vital for insect self-preservation. With multiple photoreceptors per eye, insects detect speed of movement in a way that can't be matched by bigger creatures with single-lensed eyes. A dragonfly, for instance, has up to 30,000 facets or *ommatidia* per compound eye, and processes movement so quickly that it sees the world in slow-motion.

A flower that is simply yellow to humans has markings that are clear to pollinators equipped with ultraviolet vision, guiding them straight to the nectar.

# Magnifying beauty

Although people might enjoy strong color in other aspects of their lives, when it comes to plants there is often a degree of apprehension. This is both horticultural (how will it fit in with the garden's other colors?) and cultural (it's bright orange; can I live with it?). And then there is the worry of harmonies and contrasts, and color theory in general. If the flowers on a plant seem too loud and colorful—for instance on a blood-red rhododendron—it might be because they are being grown in the wrong context. However, color is often given a free pass when it is associated with taste-makers—the "Sunset Garden" at Sissinghurst Castle is not despised, although its color palette is mainly yellow, orange, and red. At London's fastidious Chelsea Flower Show, warm golden azaleas were seen lighting up the woodland of designer Dan Pearson's Chatsworth garden, helping him to clinch the top prize of Best Garden in Show—despite being yellow.

Green is where bright colors are reconciled, since everything goes with green. There needs to be lots of it, not just in grass and trees but in plants grown mainly for their foliage, that have good shapes and textures, that move with the breeze, that are interesting in themselves. Green is rarely just green: it can be luminous and fresh, or silver-gray; variegated, or glaucous. Foliage plants do not need flowers to improve their looks: a hosta, such as the magnificent *H.* 'Empress Wu' is arguably better without its long stems of pale lilac flowers that appear in summer. For some people, vistas are the thing: straight lines with clipped evergreens that are best appreciated without the distraction of color. For others, there is the still-relevant opinion of 18th-century landscaper William Kent, that "Nature abhors a straight line."

Sneezeweed, or heleniums, offer intense color and a feast for pollinators. *Helenium* 'Sahin's Early Flowerer' works well with lots of green.

**"**There are always flowers for those who want to see them.**"**

Henri Matisse, 1947

# Plants for sight

**Peony**  *Paeonia*

"Their size and brilliancy render them striking even at a long distance," wrote William Robinson, the grandfather of naturalistic gardening—who also suggested planting peonies in grass, under trees, to be appreciated without the disappointment of a short flowering season. Woody tree peonies, raised off the ground, display their distinctive cut foliage to good effect, leaving seed heads like jester's hats. Intersectional peonies offer the best of both, at a cost.

**Early-emerging tree peonies need shelter. Herbaceous peonies must have their roots just under the surface. Fertile soil.**

**Hellebore**  *Helleborus* x *hybridus*

The color combinations can be dramatic or just sublime: purple-black with palest yellow stamens, apple green with dark red. It is worth investing in quality varieties, and allowing them to cross-pollinate (with a watchful eye, as the colors can get muddy). Remove old leaves that become coarse and brittle over the summer, revealing just the stem and elegant flower, with a small ruff of fresh leaves around the neck.

**Imitate a woodland floor by growing in shelter and part shade, in well-drained soil that is mulched to prevent drying out.**

**Red hot poker**  *Kniphofia*

This most ornamental of flowers is a lesson in context: taken out of the scorched earth of a 1970s island bed and placed amid lush, green foliage, the sunset colors sing with joy. The warm, rather than burning, hues of *Kniphofia rooperi* brighten a garden late in the season (flowering as late as October). They contrast beautifully with the jagged, glaucous foliage of *Melianthus major*, while miniature pine highlights the tubular texture of the flowers.

**Full sun, loam or sandy soil.**

**Passion flower**  *Passiflora*

Pollinated by bats and hummingbirds as well as bees and butterflies, the genus *Passiflora* consists of hundreds of species, often adapted to attract a specific pollinator. Passion flower is rightly considered a "wonder of the plant world" with rare botanical features, such as a nectar-protecting lid that only opens for pollinators that have successfully waded through the plant's pollen first. Many species, including *P. edulis*, with its familiar edible fruits, are suited to a glasshouse, while *P. caerulea* is grown outdoors.

**P. caerulea needs protection in colder areas. Full sun or part shade, fertile soil.**

Clockwise from top left *Passion flower, Hellebore, Peony, Red hot poker.*

> **"**Breeders have long tinkered with colors, ruffles, veining, and the hue of the beard, the brushlike strip along the three falls (lower petals)**"**

**Crocosmia**  *Crocosmia*

Showy sprays in late summer of glowing flowers on arching stems, each a small inflorescence of warmest red. Red 'Lucifer' is at least twice as big, and dramatic, as regular, orange crocosmia, although these African plants in the iris family share a similar arrangement of intense color over sword-shaped (and pleated) mid-green leaves. They are easily propagated by splitting the corms, which develop into joined-up chains underground. Use the freshest, which will be the top corms, for new plants.

**Full sun or part shade, moist, well-drained soil, takes some exposure.**

**Bearded iris**  *Iris germanica*

The flower structure of iris is so graphically perfect that it inspired the fleur-de-lys symbol which has endured for centuries. Although there are irises for almost every time of year and situation (from drought to pond), the stately bearded iris is the most spectacular. Visual elements are contrasted to great effect; breeders have long tinkered with colors, ruffles, veining, and the hue of the beard—the brushlike strip ranged along the three falls (lower petals).

**Plant in full sun, with excellent drainage, away from company, at a depth where the top half of the rhizomes are exposed to the sun, so that they can bake in summer.**

**Mexican sunflower**  *Tithonia rotundifolia*

Branches of fuzzily refined stems and conelike necks terminate in perfectly proportioned pumpkin-orange flowers. Warm yellow stamens complement the color of the daisylike petals on plants that are almost 6.6ft (2m) tall, showing that nature has all the best design ideas. These are half-hardy annuals, flowering from late summer until the frosts. *T. rotundifolia* 'Torch' is the preferred variety; butterflies are regular visitors.

**Sow indoors and plant out when strong enough to withstand attention from slugs.**

**Echium**  *Echium pininana*

Related to the wildflower viper's bugloss (*Echium vulgare*), the flowers were thought to resemble the venomous snake's head, and the lance-shaped, tonguelike leaves only add to this reptilian impression. *E. pininana* is the one to grow in temperate regions for its towering stature, reaching at least 13ft (4m). Self-seeding biennials, they make an informal group, like gargantuan foxgloves. The rosette of large leaves in the first year is vulnerable to frost.

Full sun, free-draining soil. Will need winter protection further north.

**Amaryllis**  *Hippeastrum*

Flowering indoors throughout winter, amaryllis brings velvety color and mesmerizing form to a quiet season. Emerging from giant bulbs, buds slowly progress upward on stout stalks, eventually erupting into spectacular flowers. Coinciding with the midwinter holiday season and Valentine's Day, they knock the socks off poinsettia, and a thoughtfully grown and cut stem would make a more imaginative (and ethical) romantic gesture than imported roses.

Grow indoors in a place that is bright but not hot. When growth picks up, keep watering. Stake with tall twigs.

**Cedar of Lebanon**  *Cedrus libani*

Majestic, horizontally arranged branches, growing to a great width and height, this grows happily on the rocky slopes of the Eastern Mediterranean and in 18th-century English landscapes. A young specimen resembles a droopy Christmas tree; it takes 50 years before it becomes a mature shape, and it still has 200 years ahead of it. Occasionally seen in incongruous places, indicating a grand country house once stood nearby. Enjoying a revival and well worth the experience of planting for the future.

Needs good drainage—and patience.

**Fritillary**  *Fritillaria*

"No plant is more decorative than the Fritillary, none more perfect in form, proportion, and embellishment," wrote artist-gardener Evelyn Dunbar, referring to snake's head fritillary, *F. meleagris*. The exterior pattern is as geometric as a checkerboard in miniature, the form is a kind of rounded box, with slender leaves and stems. They comprise a large group, including crown imperial (*F. imperialis*), flowering first, in burnt orange or yellow, and waxy Persian fritillaries (*F. persica*) on stout stems, in chic colors.

Bulbs have varying requirements, including good drainage.

Clockwise from top *Cedar of Lebanon, Fritillary, Amaryllis.*

> "A crescendo of the most spectacular crushed silk flowers in party colors—from bright salmon pink, to deep red with black blotches, to dusty pink or purple"

**Oriental poppy**  *Papaver orientalis*

The jagged foliage is among the first of the greens to perk up in spring, adding structure to a comatose border. Large, hairy, silvery buds intensity the long ascent toward flowering, with a crescendo of the most spectacular crushed silk flowers in party colors— from bright salmon pink, to deep red with black blotches, to dusty pink or purple. Cultivars are more fun than the common oriental poppy, in its fluorescent tomato soup color.

Sun or semi-shade; plant in any well-drained soil, then leave it alone. Moving leads to a long recovery, with pieces of root inevitably left behind.

**Umbrella plant**  *Darmera peltata*

The well-named umbrella plant illustrates the wonders that a structural plant can do for a garden. Mainly grown for its handsome, domed foliage with large, rounded leaves, its kinship with the Saxifrage family is revealed in late spring when pink flower clusters appear on long stems. Green leaves of 20in (50cm) wide, growing to about 3ft (1m) high, turn red in the fall before the plant disappears in winter. A hardy perennial that spreads through underground rhizomes. Divide in spring when clumps get too large.

Partial sun or full sun. Happy at water's edge or in soil that doesn't dry out.

**Molopospermum**  *Molopospermum peloponnesiacum*

If you can't pronounce the name, this is the one with pale yellow umbels on sturdy, fresh green stems, rising over frothy, fernlike leaves. These reflect light, making it a really showy plant. Foliage is wide, needing about 3ft (1m) around, with a height of about 5ft (1.5m). *M. peloponnesiacum* is a hardy perennial, and, like all umbellifers (parsley family-members with flowers arranged in umbels), the seeds are best sown fresh, in the fall, at the time when the plant would naturally be propagating on its own.

Part shade preferable, well-drained, moisture-retentive soil, plenty of space.

Left *Oriental poppy.*

**Water lily**  *Nymphaea*

A highly ornamental plant that is not difficult to place, as every garden benefits from having some kind of container of water. A pygmy water lily would suit a deep bowl or mini pond, while medium and large varieties offer a wider range of colors, with elegantly mottled leaves, streaked or spotted in red against green, or simply a solid dark red. They offer shade to submerged frogs, attract dragonflies, and discourage algae by withholding light.

Leaves die down to the underwater rhizomes in winter. In summer, cut spent flowers and leaves below the water surface.

**Crimson glory vine**  *Vitis coignetiae*

An oversized vine, with platters of leaves that are veined in close-up and pleasantly lobed from a distance, *Vitis coignetiae* lights up in the fall, mixing bright and muted reds with green. Glory vine clothes its support rather than smothering it. Growing against the warm hues of a sandstone or ironstone building, the effect is enhanced, but it can also be pressed into service as a coverer of less attractive supports. It is vigorous and needs its own space.

Appreciates sun or semi-shade, in any kind of soil as long as it is well-drained.

**Tetrapanax**  *Tetrapanax papyrifer*

Theatrical treelike plants grown for giant, clawed-hand leaves on stems that can be 13ft (4m) tall. Tetrapanax has a will to live: it can be evergreen, deciduous, or perennial, depending on the degree of cold. It can be invasive (please check for your area), but, in less hospitable climes, these Taiwan natives make an extraordinary backdrop against the north side of a building, and, kept in check, as part of a textural exotic garden. Brown stems and undersides of leaves are handsomely hirsute.

Sheltered sun or partial shade.

**African lily**  *Agapanthus*

After all the blues and purples of spring, agapanthus brings a welcome shot of intense indigo in summer, or a choice of paler blues and whites. They are sturdy, strong, and glamorous, particularly in rows of large containers. Agapanthus is good news for anyone without a garden, as growing them in pots allows for more tender varieties, to be taken inside in winter. Often growing to more than 5ft (1.5m), with well-proportioned, strappy leaves: they have advantages over the alliums of spring.

Perform well with some root restriction, and good drainage. Repot if root-bound.

Clockwise from top *Water lily, Tetrapanax, African lily.*

# SOUND

The orchestra of outdoors is most clamorous
from animals, but plants add the *chiaroscuro*
sounds. The quality of a breeze affects the
timbre of their rustling: a tingle from birch, with
its small leaves and pliable branches; a louder
susurration from bamboo. When a summer
storm whooshes through trees in full leaf, it
is more unsettling, roaring like the sea. What
will the damage be? Insects and birds are more
regular. When a cricket is in full song, it is
possible, by listening and doing a bit of math,
to divine the ambient temperature, as its chirps
increase with heat. It is the sounds of courting
and protecting territory that provide the regular
soundscape of the warmer months.

Birch makes a soft noise and
casts a light shadow.

# Ideas on sound and song in a garden

When your part of the Earth wakes up in spring, gardens are noisy once more. Not everyone experiences the sharp contrast between the muffled sounds of snow-bound late winter and the clarion notes of early spring, but a sense of anticipation is universal when new greenery emerges. After spurts of watery sunshine, the first fully warm day throws outdoor noises into relief: the vibrating "zizz, bizz, bizzz" of a bumblebee (to quote Beatrix Potter), or the piercing soprano of a robin. They are more noticeable because you are suddenly positioning yourself outside, maybe for the first time in months. Some birds twitter; crows might caw—if it is continuous and it's coming from the air, it could be a hawk circling around their nests. Or you may hear a red-shouldered hawk emitting a high-pitched whistle while it's being "mobbed" by an oriole who is shooing it away from its territory.

**Spring's in session**

When the sun shines, people size up their hedges, reaching for their power tools. Where a lawnmower has the low rumble of routine, hedge-cutting can be antisocial and is ideally done on a weekday. Cars are vacuumed and power-washed; dogs become more vocal than before. In the fall, a leaf blower does the excessively noisy (and polluting) job of blowing leaves from one place to another. As the late Duchess of Devonshire put it, "The garden is no longer a place for quiet contemplation." An advantage of having a plot smaller than the acreage of an English manor—and not open to the general public—is that there are no rules. Fighting nature with an armory of tools and potions is a bother that is largely self-inflicted. Working *with* it is more likely to be more successful, more satyisfying—and involve less effort.

As well as new colors and fresh growth, a spring garden is alive with sound. Insects reemerge, people go outside, and birds return from distant places.

### The orchestra of outdoors

In March, early-blossoming plants, such as crocuses, make a distant hum, getting louder and busier on approach: it is clear that these beautiful flowers have caught the attention of the local bees. If you sit quietly in spring (without looking at a mobile phone) there are "micro sounds" that are worth noticing. You can physically hear shrubs turning green: papery leaves land on the ground after a gust of wind separates the dangling winter coverings of hornbeam or beech, just as spring buds push them off. Beech leaves make a particular clatter on paving or gravel. In the fall, large trees of beech are equally noisy—and beautiful to watch—as they shower down, in shades of bronze, over a couple of days, shinier and harder and therefore louder than most deciduous foliage. Swooshing through deep piles of leaves is a pleasure that no one grows out of.

Of all the senses that are alerted when outdoors, sounds are the most obviously atmospheric. Music in a garden is an occasional joy—a quartet playing in a grassy amphitheater, a group of folk singers at a county fair—but the other, nonstop orchestra takes place every day and night. Nocturnal noises are enchanting when heard from the safety of your bed; an owl hooting, rain against glass, a strange bark from a fox or racoon (or is it a wolf?). Scratching from the attic is not so good, or any sign of wild animals in the wrong place, from a butterfly flapping against a lampshade, to a bird or bat lurching in every direction except for the open window. It is not only animals that provide the tempo and pitch of outdoors: a distant thwacking of a ball, clapping, children's shrieks, all are sounds of people unclenching. Winter shivering is replaced by summer basking, and it is audible.

Beech, oak, and American chestnut are all from the same tree family (*Fagaceae*) and they have thick leaves in common that clatter on to the ground. The shells of beech nuts add extra crunch in the fall.

At the dawn of a new day, animals relish the time that they have to themselves, when people are generally in bed. Driving around the countryside at 5am in summer reveals rabbits or racoons taking over the roads, with foxes and deer in less of a rush than usual. Pigeons in the road take barely any notice of vehicles at all.

In early spring, a walk near any kind of wooded pond or lake could reveal a chorus of bleating lambs and the guttural sounds of their mothers, joined by crows, a pheasant croak and a sudden beating of wings, a heron hollering, a moorhen chattering—both echoing somewhat between the water and the trees. This is the way to hear a nightingale, if you ever wondered what the famous gurgling song is really like. Unidentified splashes and plops bring the attention back to water; it is blissfully immersive and all that is required is that you get there before anyone else does.

## The art of slowing down

Stopping to listen is a way of pulling up and coming to a standstill. Listening, as opposed to hearing, is quite difficult to do in a hurry. When nature's sounds are allowed to get through, they take on a symbolism that marks time, and celebrates the moment. The easily identified cuckoo's call, or the distinctive whistle-trill from the beautiful cardinal, will stop you in your tracks, if this is the first time you've heard them since the previous year. It's the aural equivalent of the first swallow, when it is newly arrived from distant continents, promising halcyon days to come.

In Japan, an acknowledgment of imperfection and transience (*wabi-sabi*), that is honored in lingering detail, has for centuries been an important concept of beauty.

Nature strongly informs Japanese aesthetics and traditions, even though very few people now live in the countryside (less than 10 percent of the country's total population). This is why the traditional Japanese calendar of 72 seasons still has traction, and deserves to be adapted elsewhere. Instead of the familiar long and somewhat amorphous markers of spring, summer, fall, and winter in the west, Japanese microseasons (*kō*), progress every five days or so. Their names are poetic in their economy. Seasons to listen out for include: "distant thunder" (end of March–beginning of April), "frogs start singing" (early May), and "crickets chirp around the door" (third week of October).

## Winged chorus

The degree of sonic hum coming from invertebrates and frogs is louder on different continents; North America is lucky enough to have a full complement of crickets, katydids, grasshoppers, and singing frogs, as well as hummingbirds whirring around nectar-rich flowers. Residents of southern Europe are used to shouting over the noise of annual cicadas, or dodging out of the flight path of a droning (and diurnal) hummingbird hawk-moth. Northern climes are quieter, with birdsong coming to the fore, and the occasional cameo appearance from big, flying beetles such as the cockchafer (or May bug), crashing around the place in early summer. In bird and insect life, "music" is really the sound of territory being staked and protected, and it's generally a sign of virility. The 100-decibel scratching sound of a single cicada comes from the male's drum-like tymbals (a part of the exoskeleton, in the abdomen), while a cricket's staccato chirp and a grasshopper's continuous, silvery sound come from the

"Frogs start singing" marks one of the 72 microseasons in the Japanese calendar, lasting for about five days, until the next evocatively named season comes along.

process of stridulation, the sound of a plectrum (hind leg) being dragged across a stridulitrum (forewing), in the manner of a stringed instrument. Ants also stridulate.

Birds bring squawking and shrieks to a garden, as well as melody, of course. A starling, at its most musical, makes bubbling sounds from rooftops but betrays its dinosaur origins as it screeches in flight, crashing onto a bird feeder. In spring, the cacophony of hungry starlings is amplified as young, puffed-up fledglings push the adults into feeding them as fast as possible, with a predator-attracting kerfuffle.

A grasshopper stridulating away in high summer. The back leg is dragged across the forewing in the manner of a violin bow or guitar plectrum.

Birds (and insects) need to feel safe in order to sing; notice how a cricket becomes silent as you walk toward it and continues as soon as you've passed. A gang of garrulous sparrows on a vine-covered pergola will stop chattering and fly away when they see an unfamiliar person approaching, but if this regular hangout is in your garden, they will soon learn to ignore you. When sparrows choose your garden as a gathering place, there is regular chattering every morning and afternoon, spring or winter. Sparrows like a place that is a little unruly (barely pruned, rambling roses are perfect). They depend on a functioning food chain; gardening for birds is seamlessly connected with gardening for insects, mammals, and amphibians.

**Silence**

An owl flies and eats silently. White barn owls aside, they are usually difficult to see and must remain invisible to their prey. Owls swallow their victims all at once, since it would be counterproductive to loudly crunch and chew. By day, an awkward flapping and honking and flying around in circles is the signal of swans in flight, and pheasants look almost as ill-suited to taking to the air. A peacock's unearthly meow, at any time of day or night, setting off other peacocks in a tuneless chorus, will make you an unpopular neighbor if you harbor dreams of a pleasure garden roamed by exotic birds. Eerie night noises are banished by the regular and repetitive crowing of a cockerel, by turns soothing and irritating. In *Hamlet*, the harsh cries of a cockerel even manage to banish the ghost, "The trumpet to the morn, / Doth with his lofty and shrill-sounding throat / Awake the god of day."

# The dawn chorus

As a morning wake-up call, what could be better than the dawn chorus? It begins a bit too early, with auroral birdsong reaching a crescendo at around daybreak. It is most intense about a month before the summer solstice, so if you have trees and shrubs nearby, there could be a very loud noise outside your window by 4:30am. In temperate countries, a blackbird is often the first soloist, followed by a robin, and then the full chorus, with wrens and finches joining in as light increases. Get up early, and, once in a season, see what it's like being immersed in this wall of life-enhancing sound.

Standing and listening, near water and trees, will reveal the sounds of mourning doves and crows, also perhaps an owl, pheasant, ducks—all easily recognizable. A birdsong app on your phone could be the best thing you have on there, helping you to identify the songs of less familiar birds, such as orioles, treecreepers, blackcap chickadees, and, on a good day, a nightingale. Song thrush is one of the most melodious of songbirds; recognizing its stock of musical phrases is comforting in one's own outdoor space, since song thrushes eat snails, whacking their shells against a stone (and illustrating why slug pellets are a terrible idea).

A robin, bursting into his or her shrill song. Both male and female robins sing, and physically are near-impossible to distinguish.

### When birds seem to disappear

After midsummer, the first brood of chicks will have hatched and left the nest, and there is less need of territory-defending. Birds run out of reasons to be competitively vocal. By late summer, things turn noticeably quiet. Birds start to molt, impeding their ability to fly, so they hide from predators during the process. As the natural bounty of berries, seeds, and fruits ripen, birds have less use for bird feeders, mainly returning to gardens after the first frosts.

# The science of sound

Hearing is intensely physical: sound is relayed from a vibrating source to the inner ear, with the aid of molecules that keep the vibrations moving. Gathering momentum as they travel through air, water, or even a wooden fence, these vibrating particles develop into sound waves, which collect in a person's proverbial "shell-like" ear. The outer ear is shaped a bit like a seashell, while the inner ear—or cochlea—more strongly resembles the shell of a snail, complete with fluid to smooth the passage of vibrating sound. Before reaching this point, sound molecules are funneled down the ear canal, hitting the ear drum and setting off three little bones, vividly known as the hammer, anvil, and stirrup. Sound is constantly in motion as it is processed by the auditory nerve and finally the brain. It travels about a million times less quickly than light, which is why we hear thunder after seeing lightning.

Regarding life on Earth, it is instructive to realize how much comes down to vibrations. In space, where there are no air particles, no noise is emitted or heard. When plants react to music, they do not show a preference for a certain genre, although they are sensitive to high frequency and decibel levels. Plants' reactions to noises are based on vibrations. The buzzing of a bumblebee (whose whole body vibrates as it bumbles around), instigates an increase in pollen production in some plants, while the vibrations of a herbivore's teeth or mandibles tearing into its neighbors triggers defense chemicals. Just as scientists are beginning to investigate the possibilities of harnessing good vibrations for increased plant health, so we as a race are slowly learning to appreciate that the sounds of the natural world can also be good for us to listen to.

It is quite likely that foxgloves love the sound of buzzing bees.

# Amplifying the sounds that you like

Pleasant sounds are generally not intrusive, so we don't always notice them, even though a blackbird might be singing a ravishing song. To make us sit up and listen, it can take a full choir of birds, or the sudden, high-voltage aria of a tiny wren. In a garden, the ear leads the eye to the bird, and robins in particular will sing from the same nearby branch, day after day. It is our job to create more safe places from which birds can sing—and this could be as easy as allowing a formal hedge to go a bit shaggy (this is very nice with hornbeam or beech), or planting small trees near a preferred place to sit, rather than choosing the shade of an unwieldy umbrella.

A garden that is home to birds will have places for them to sleep. Birds naturally rest in hedges and evergreen shrubs; cavity-dwelling birds use holes in trees. For them, the nesting box of spring doubles up as a roosting box in winter, with small birds piling in for warmth. Be a good custodian and clean out any bird boxes that you have after August. Birds have evolved to survive without help, but since we as a species encroach on their livelihoods, we could at least make things easier for them. A brush pile will provide pockets for sheltering birds: bear this in mind when wondering what to do with the spent Christmas tree. Dismember it, and along with branches from other tree and hedge thinnings, put it all behind a shed and forget about it—until next year, when you add more. A tidy wood pile that is in constant use is more for people than for smaller creatures, so try to leave certain out-of-the-way areas unswept and untidied.

Crepuscular rustling is delightful, not creepy, if you discover there are hedgehogs in the vicinity. Like any animal, a hedgehog prefers a garden that is not trying too hard. When people talk about an outdoor "room," there is an urge to make

A song thrush, enjoying the cover that this garden provides, as well as a freshly dug worm. Thrushes are great guzzlers of snails and slugs.

it just that: a sitting room outdoors, in which an all-weather rug and floor lamps are the first steps toward fake grass and plastic topiary that bleaches blue in the sun. It is so much easier not to bother with these things, and save the expense. By planting or enhancing a mix of trees, climbers, hedges, choice evergreen shrubs, areas of long grass, and small pools of water, you will look like a good gardener (no matter how much you insist you don't have time to garden) because you have put in a few quality items, the sort that live and breathe.

One of the advantages of hedges, besides providing food and shelter for birds, mammals, and insects, is that they absorb sound. Inherently annoying noises such as dogs' squeaky toys are better tolerated if you like the dogs and people that they belong to, but the ability to reduce the reminders of others is an advantage if your garden is going to become any kind of haven. The deeper the hedge the better, but, realistically, an evergreen hedge such as holly or cherry laurel could be fronted with further evergreen shrubs, for instance loosely shaped box or common yew. Flower color in between will benefit from the structure.

Conversely, gravel accentuates noise, being a natural intruder-alert, and it is a growing medium that is very attractive to plants, keeping their roots cool and aiding drainage. Sounds are also good at combating other sounds: trickling water will drown out the minutiae of a neighbor's conversation, while a gushing fountain will obliterate them. In northern climates, rushing water is invigorating but not very relaxing. A slight gurgle is far more attractive to insect life, and, once again, the reliable garden soundtrack: birds.

The presence of water is probably the single most effective way of inviting bird and animal life, and therefore layers of sound, into your garden. If it trickles, all the better.

"I value my garden more for being full of blackbirds than cherries, and very frankly give them fruit for their songs."

Joseph Addison, 1712

# Plant profiles: sound

**Noninvasive bamboo**  *Fargesia*
**or** *Phyllostachys*

If you like the sounds that wind
activates, bamboo is a more subtle,
growing, wind chime, with rustling
leaves and jostling stems. Be sure
to choose a variety of bamboo that is
right for your climate: for example,
*Fargesia* does not do well in excessive
heat. In the north, the cold-hardiness
rating needs to be within your winter
temperature range.

Keep moist while establishing. Surround it
with an underground barrier.

**Fig**  *Ficus carica*

Growing in the manner of a large
shrub, with branches and leaves
reaching down to the ground, fig trees
are always rustling, since they attract
more animals than any other fruit tree,
anywhere. Whether the rootling comes
from a hedgehog or a tortoise, there are
more than 1,000 mammals and birds
that eat figs, and they are both diurnal
and nocturnal. To combine ecology
with elegance, grow a fanned-out
fig tree against a south- or west-facing
wall.

For better fruit, restrict roots, on planting
in full sun. Hardy varieties will thrive when
planted further north.

**Weeping beech, birch, and willow**

Weeping trees bring theater to a garden,
with curtains of branches reaching all
the way down to the ground. Standing
next to, or inside, the canopy of a
weeper, large or small, is as immersive
as a tree experience gets. The pliable
branches are easily set in motion with
the slightest breeze, from giant weeping
willow or weeping beech (its fall leaves
bearing all the changing colors at once),
while a small weeping birch or acer
makes a more diaphanous rustle.

Young trees do best when planted small,
with regular irrigation in the early years.

**Sweet corn**  *Zea mays*

Corn on the cob is impossible to eat
quietly. Perfectly ripe and cooked,
kernels pop and ping between the teeth,
each bite joyously audible and best
done in a group. Purists insist that corn
cobs must be roasted in their husks on a
grill outdoors. This way, everyone can
join in the noisy business of shucking,
or pulling off the papery wrapping and
silky strands. Buttering, adding salt, and
handling corn without burning the
fingers is sociable, chattering fun.

Relies on wind for pollination so is best
grown in blocks instead of rows; sustained
sunshine is needed for ripening.

Right *Fig.*

# "The sound of air currents meeting birch in other seasons creates a laughing, whispering, or chattering"

### Silver birch   *Betula pendula*

A gentle breeze through a light canopy of small leaves on pliable stems is cheering, and subtly different in tone through the seasons. Ivan Turgenev, in his short story *The Rendezvous*, describes a grove of birch trees with a breeze coasting over the top of them during the first weeks of September. The sound of air currents meeting birch in other seasons creates a laughing, whispering, or chattering, but this is "a barely audible, drowsy prattle." Take Turgenev's lead and mark the seasons with conversational birch.

**Any aspect or soil that is well-drained, in sun or semi-shade.**

### Common sunflower   *Helianthus annuus*

Sunflowers are the most graphic of plants: tall stalk, big sunny flower. For introducing children to the delights of a buzzing and twittering garden, these annuals are pleasingly fast-growing. Bumblebees will clamber over the small tubular flowers that make up the oversized flowerhead, pollen sticking to their bodies as they go. In the fall, these dinner plates are packed with sunflower seeds in the most efficient way, pulling in cardinals, nuthatches, and twittering goldfinches.

**Shelter, full sun, and moist but well-drained soil. Be prepared to tie them to something solid as they grow—and grow.**

### Apple   *Malus domestica*

An apple tree is excellent value in a garden and it is among the noisiest of fruits. Using a knife to eat a ripe apple has an anticipatory resonance, but this is outweighed by the joy of cracking into one, with teeth and jaw, magnified by the proximity of mouth and ears. Subsequent bites diminish in effect, but, as a ritual of noise, it is hard to ignore— not to mention the decadent sound of the fruit dropping from the highest, unreachable branches onto hard turf.

**Grow in a sunny, sheltered position, in well-drained loam.**

**Honesty**  *Lunaria annua*

Despite the Latin name, honesty is often biennial, and, as with biennial foxgloves, they are such an agreeable presence in a garden that it is worth sowing their seeds two years running, to ensure a continuous supply. Flowering in purple-mauve or white, all honesties share the same papery seed cases— translucent planes stretched taut on an oval frame. They rattle pleasantly in the breeze, or in retro flower arrangements. Equally good value before this stage, as the seed pods develop.

**Very easy-going in moist but well-drained soil; any aspect except north-facing.**

**Crab apple**  *Malus*

Being in the rose family (*Rosaceae*), crab apple scores with all garden senses. Crab apples are important trees for wildlife, attracting birds that are among the most vocal of garden songsters. Generally medium-sized, crab apples are well-suited to planting near a window, giving a year-long perch for blackbirds, song thrushes, and robins, whose song emerges from pretty pink or white blossoms in spring. The fleshy fruits are choice food in the fall.

**Full sun for the best fruit and any soil that is moist and well-drained.**

**Silver grass**  *Miscanthus sinensis 'Morning Light'*

Grasses have a wonderful swishing sound in a breeze, as well as being irresistibly touchable, when they are soft or silky. Miscanthus has a perfectly rustling, long stem but it is not possible to recommend all of them, due to the behavior of non-natives in different climates. *Miscanthus sinensis* 'Morning Light' is clump-forming, and is used by garden designers in temperate climates for its moderate behavior, also catching the light well, to add to its sensual attributes.

**Long-lasting in winter; prune in spring.**

**Cotoneaster**  *Cotoneaster horizontalis*

Since plants are at the bottom of several food chains, consider them as a means of bringing the hustle and bustle of life into your garden. Shrubs with berries attract insects, birds, and mammals, with fallen fruit that enriches the earth. Blackbirds are mainly ground feeders and their keen hearing detects worms underground. *Cotoneaster horizontalis* makes a handsome, low-growing tracery of black twigs with red berries, with birds hopping all over them in winter.

**Sun or part shade, moist well-drained soil; works well with architecture.**

Clockwise from top left *Honesty, Crab apple, Silver grass.*

# "A stout hedge will do the job of sequestering noise pollution (as well as capturing carbon)"

**Greater quaking grass**  *Briza maxima*

They are just as light-catching and tactile as they are jingly-jangly—a must for flower decorators. Hanging in groups and held aloft as if on a fishing rod, the pale pupalike flower heads are the source of delicate clacking sounds when they are handled. Only growing to about 2ft (60cm) high, they have weedlike tendencies on well-drained soil, and resemble ordinary grass before the buds form. In a garden they work best when corraled into a designated cutting garden.

Any aspect, any soil, with moisture preferred. Happy in exposed locations.

**Common holly**  *Ilex aquifolium*

While specimen holly trees are wonderful, a hedge of holly is a top sound-absorber. A stout hedge will do the job of sequestering noise pollution (as well as capturing carbon) and the deeper the hedge, the more effective the sound barrier. This is good news for anyone who has the space, since both male and female trees are required for berry production. Branches will reach down to the ground, offering good cover all year round and a stout shelter for small animals.

Hardy. Grows well in woodland, in semi-shade, or in full sun. Any well-drained soil.

**Euphorbia**  *Euphorbia*

This massive genus is important to explore for a textured, year-round garden. Fluorescent green flowers in spring are characteristic of many varieties, such as popular *Euphorbia characias* subsp. *wulfenii*, followed by prominent seed heads. Seeds of caper spurge (*Euphorbia lathyris*) darken as they ripen, resembling capers, before being catapulted into the air. The sound, like the double click of a camera shutter, is arresting, a belated reminder to cut plants back before this stage, as seeds are dispersed away from the space occupied by the parent plant.

Sun to partial shade, prefers fertile, well-drained soil.

**Californian lilac**  *Ceanothus*

"To dehisce" is one way of describing what a ceanothus seed capsule does when the seeds are ripe and ready to disperse. The ovary pings off and seeds are ejected in a small explosion, not the most efficient way of propagating, and unlikely to create a ceanothus forest in your garden. Buy a named cultivar that is suited to your conditions (they are mostly native to California) and marvel at the unmissable buzzing from this woody shrub when it bursts into clusters of small, intensely-hued blue-purple flowers in early summer.

**Good drainage essential, it has some drought tolerance. Requires full sun and shelter.**

**Bladder campion**  *Silene vulgaris*

The leaves and stalks squeak when you rub them together. This could be reason enough for growing them, although if you lived in Umbria you might like them in a regional pasta sauce, too. The structure of the plant resembles a simple campion, with a bike horn pump behind the flower head, or "bladder," which is ridged. If you have any rough ground, with chalky or sandy soil, this could join wildflowers in long grass.

**They are wildflowers and thrive on exposure and sun to semi-shade.**

**Whistling jacks**  *Gladiolus communis* subsp. *byzantinus*

The musical leaves, wider than grass and therefore louder, have given Byzantine gladioli their nickname of "whistling jacks." Native to Sicily and southern Spain but now found worldwide, they are prized for the noise they make when a leaf is placed between two straight thumbs and blown through, honking like a slightly hysterical bird. Grown-up gardeners appreciate their intense magenta flowers on long stems, better mixers than florists' gladioli.

**Full sun, good drainage; grow in a border or naturalize in long grass.**

**Opium poppy**  *Papaver somniferum*

One of the best things about this is its seed head, a rounded pepper pot with an ornate lid. As the glaucous color fades, a poppy retains its structure, standing tall until the stem gives way and it falls. The seeds swish inside the case for months, dispersed from the little holes near the top by wind, or people who are fascinated by the convenience of this design, shaking seeds where they want them to land.

**Will grow anywhere with good drainage; thin out the seedlings.**

*Right from top to bottom* Whistling jacks, Opium poppy.

# Index

## About the author

**Kendra Wilson** is the author of nine books on gardens and art. Her journalism career was bookended by British *Vogue* and *The Observer*, with a stint at Condé Nast in New York, and a design degree at Central Saint Martins, in between. On moving to the English countryside, Kendra became a reporter of gardens, while working as an undergardener at ancient estates in Northamptonshire. A regular contributor to *Gardens Illustrated* and other glossy garden monthlies, her most fervent interest is to draw attention to imaginatively conceived spaces, in which design and horticulture work with nature, rather than against it.

## Acknowledgments

The author would like to thank everyone involved with DK who smoothed the path of this book, and Chris Young for setting it in motion. Special thanks to Lucy Bannell, wonder editor. For sharing aspects of their gardens: James Alexander-Sinclair, Claudio Bincoletto and Keythorpe Walled Garden, Tania Compton, Damson Farm, Izi Glover, Hampton Court Castle, Arne Maynard Garden Design, Saint Timothee, Salthrop House, Simon Spence and Worton Kitchen Garden. Also to Anna Benn, Celestria Alexander-Sinclair, and Happy Cat Farm, Pennsylvania.

## Publisher Acknowledgments

Dorling Kindersley would like to thank Kathy Steer for proofreading, Vanessa Bird for indexing, and Steve Crozier for repro work.

## Picture credits

A heartfelt thanks to the photographers who have brought so much to this small volume.

(Key: a-above; b-below/bottom; c-centre; f-far; l-left; r-right; t-top)

All photography by **Britt Willoughby Dyer** except for:

**4-5 Andrew Maybury. 13 Jim Powell. 27 GAP Photos:** Heather Edwards. **30 Dreamstime.com:** Ammentorp. **39 Andrew Maybury. 41 Kendra Wilson:** (br). **42 Andrew Maybury:** (br). **Jim Powell:** (t). **46 GAP Photos:** Jonathan Buckley (br). **Kendra Wilson:** (bl). **49 GAP Photos:** Robert Mabic (tl). **50 Andrew Maybury. 53 GAP Photos. 63 Andrew Maybury. 65 Valery Rizzo. 66 Valery Rizzo. 71 GAP Photos:** Christa Brand (tr). **Jim Powell:** (tl). **Valery Rizzo:** (b). **72 Alamy Stock Photo:** Inga Spence (t). **Valery Rizzo:** (b). **76 GAP Photos:** Jonathan Buckley (tl, tr). **Shutterstock. com:** Milan Sommer (b). **79 Andrew Maybury:** (br, bl). **80 Andrew Maybury. 90-91 Jim Powell. 102 Andrew Maybury. 105 GAP Photos:** Jonathan Buckley (br). **Andrew Maybury:** (bl). **106 GAP Photos:** Jonathan Buckley (tl). **113 Jim Powell. 123 Andrew Maybury. 131 Andrew Maybury:** (br). **Jim Powell:** (bl). **132 Andrew Maybury:** (t). **Jim Powell:** (bl). **135 Alamy Stock Photo:** foto-bee (t). **GAP Photos:** Jonathan Buckley (bl). **148 Andrew Maybury. 150 GAP Photos:** Gary Smith. **153 Andrew Maybury. 159 Dreamstime. com:** Amani A. **162 Andrew Maybury:** (t). **165 Alamy Stock Photo:** Botanic World (b). **166 GAP Photos:** Dianna Jazwinski (br). **169 Jim Powell:** (b).

Penguin
Random
House

| | |
| --- | --- |
| **Project Editor** | Lucy Bannell |
| **US Editor** | Karyn Gerhard |
| **Designer** | Tessa Bindloss |
| **Senior Designer** | Barbara Zuniga |
| **Picture Research** | Kendra Wilson |
| **Editorial Manager** | Ruth O'Rourke |
| **Design Manager** | Marianne Markham |
| **Jacket Design** | Maxine Pedliham |
| **Jackets Coordinator** | Lucy Philpott |
| **Pre-production Producer** | David Almond |
| **Senior Producer** | Rebecca Parton |
| **Creative Technical Support** | Sonia Charbonnier |
| **Art Director** | Maxine Pedliham |
| **Publishing Director** | Katie Cowan |

First American Edition, 2022
Published in the United States by DK Publishing
1450 Broadway, Suite 801, New York, NY 10018

Copyright © 2022 Dorling Kindersley Limited
DK, a Division of Penguin Random House LLC
22 23 24 25 26  10 9 8 7 6 5 4 3 2 1
001–326296–Feb/2022

A catalog record for this book is available from the Library of Congress.
ISBN 978-0-7440-4806-3

DK books are available at special discounts when purchased in bulk for sales
promotions, premiums, fund-raising, or educational use. For details, contact:
DK Publishing Special Markets, 1450 Broadway, Suite 801, New York, NY 10018

SpecialSales@dk.com

Printed and bound in China

## For the curious
**www.dk.com**

This book was made with Forest Stewardship
Council™ certified paper—one small step in DK's
commitment to a sustainable future. For more
information go to www.dk.com/our-green-pledge